T0319224

The Pandemic and Social Science Approaches to Teaching and Learning

Editors

Maheshvari Naidu • Vivian Ojong

Publisher:
Langaa RPCIG
Langaa Research & Publishing Common Initiative Group
P.O. Box 902 Mankon
Bamenda
North West Region
Cameroon
Langaagrp@gmail.com
www.langaa-rpcig.net

Distributed in and outside N. America by African Books Collective
orders@africanbookscollective.com
www.africanbookscollective.com

ISBN-10: 9956-552-71-2
ISBN-13: 978-9956-552-71-9

© Maheshvari Naidu and Vivian Ojong 2023

Chellan, Noel

Noel Chellan is currently an academic in the Department of Sociology in the School of Social Sciences at the University of KwaZulu-Natal in Durban, South Africa. His teaching interests include environmental and developmental issues and society – more especially South African society. His research areas have thus far focused on ecotourism in South Africa, energy-poverty in rural South Africa, land and livelihood challenges confronting indigenous communities, violence in schools, and energy and social change. He holds a PhD in Ecotourism (geography and environmental sciences) from the University of KwaZulu-Natal.

Govender, Subashini

Subashini Govender has a PhD in Sociology from the University of KwaZulu-Natal. Her work is in the area of Diasporic Indian identities. She has taught courses in Sociology over the last several years as a contract lecturer. She has also worked as a research assistant on a large Humanities Project and will shortly take up a prestigious post-doctoral scholarship.

Johnson, Belinda

Belinda Johnson is a lecturer at the University of KwaZulu-Natal. She is currently teaching in the International and Public Affairs Cluster and is the Programme Coordinator for the Public Policy Programme. She teaches in both the Public Policy Programme and Conflict Transformation and Peace Studies. Her areas of expertise cover public policy design and analysis, implementation and project management, monitoring and evaluation and research methodology and methods for policy research. These includes research on the following areas: higher education in South Africa, environmental policy design and implementation in South Africa, political communication, human rights and international public law, and labour law and legislation in South Africa she is currently completing her PhD.

Mhandu, John

John Mhandu is a postdoctoral fellow at the University of KwaZulu-Natal, School of Social Science, Sociology Department. He is a self-motivated and results-driven intellectual with a background in social theory and research methodology (both qualitative and quantitative)]. He has written on issues of migration, informality, informal economy, and social change. He has ten (10) years of experience at leading South African universities, teaching and mentoring student from various social and cultural backgrounds. He received prestigious postgraduate merit awards from the University of the Witwatersrand and University of Pretoria for outstanding performance.

Naidu, Maheshvari

Maheshvari Naidu is a Full Professor in Social Anthropology. She is widely published in gender and wider social science journals focusing on a diverse range of anthropological issues linked to religion and gender, body politic, ritual and power, LBGTQI identities and spirituality. She has supervised a large cohort of Postgraduate students and Post-Doctoral Fellows and has graduated 15 Masters and 23 Doctoral Students. She is on the board of the journal *Anthropology Southern Africa and AlterNation*. Her research has a feminist approach and is located amongst South African Black women and other marginalised populations. More recently, her work has moved to interdisciplinary collaborations, which she relishes. All her project collaborations aim to contribute to social cohesion, and focus on South African socio-cultural realities.

Ojong, Vivian

Vivian Ojong is a Full Professor of Anthropology in the School of Social Sciences at the University of KwaZulu-Natal. She is also the Dean and Head of School of Social Sciences. She is widely published and has written on diverse issues of ethnography, gender and fieldwork, religion and migration, globalization and diaspora studies, gender, the politics of identity, knowledge production, African feminism, entrepreneurship, culture and religion and identity politics. Her multidisciplinary approach is demonstrated through her co-authored publications with colleagues from other disciplinary background. She has graduated a large number of masters and doctoral students.

Pillay, Kathryn

Kathryn Pillay is a Senior Lecturer in Sociology at the University of KwaZulu-Natal (UKZN), South Africa. She holds a PhD in Sociology from UKZN. Her areas of teaching and research include that of 'race', migration, identity and belonging. Her most recent publication is the co-edited volume, *Relating Worlds of Racism – Dehumanisation, Belonging and the Normativity of European Whiteness* (Palgrave Macmillan, 2019), which unmasks and foregrounds the ways in which notions of European whiteness have found form in a variety of global contexts that continue to sustain racism as an operational norm resulting in exclusion, violence, human rights violations, isolation and limited full citizenship for individuals who are not racialised as white.

Rieker, Mark

Mark Rieker is a lecturer in Policy and Development Studies in the School of Social Sciences at the University of KwaZulu-Natal. He has taught in the fields of sociology, public policy analysis, methodology and the management of public policy. His research interests include policy implementation, policy networks and the link between social media and good governance. He has also worked in the area of access to higher education and specifically the development of pedagogical and assessment approaches for student success.

Ruggunan, Shaun

Shaun Ruggunan is a Professor of Human Resources Management at the University of KwaZulu-Natal in Durban, South Africa. Shaun's Ph.D. in Industrial, Organisational and Labour Studies looked at the agency of maritime labours in a globalising world. His research focuses on maritime labour markets and how organised labour is an agent of globalisation. More recently, Shaun's work is on decolonising management studies in South Africa. Shaun has published two well-received books. The first book, *Waves of Change: Globalisation and Seafaring Labour Markets* (2016: HSRC Press), and his second book, with R. Sooryamoorthy, *Management Studies in South Africa: Examining the Trajectory in the Apartheid Era and Beyond* (Palgrave, 2019) both further unpack his ideas in his research areas. Additionally, Shaun has served as guest editor of a number of journals including, *South African Review of Sociology, Organization and Professions and Professionalism.*

Shoko, Evans

Evans Shoko is a Postdoctoral Researcher with the Andrew Mellon Foundation Spatial Humanities Project in the College of Humanities, University of KwaZulu-Natal. He holds a PhD in Conflict Transformation and Peace Studies. He is multidisciplinary in his approach. His research interests are in water management, positive peace, community participation and socially constructed spaces. He has a diversity of methodological experience in both quantitative and qualitative approaches. He has extensive teaching and supervisory experience at the undergraduate and postgraduate levels.

Vahed, Goolam

Goolam Vahed received his PhD from Indiana University, Bloomington, USA, and is currently a Professor in the Department of History at the University of KwaZulu-Natal. He has published widely on identity formation, citizenship, ethnicity, migration and transnationalism among Indian South Africans, as well as the role of sport and culture in South African society. He has published in peer-reviewed journals, while his most recent co-authored books include *Schooling Muslims in Natal: Identity, State and the Orient Islamic Educational Institute; The South African Gandhi. Stretcher-Bearer of Empire; Chota Motala. A Biography of Political Activism in the KwaZulu-Natal Midlands*; and *A History of the Present. A Biography of Indian South Africans*, 1994–2019, which was published by Oxford University Press in 2019.

Table of Contents

It gives me immense pleasure to write this short preface to this book.

Birthed in the context of pedagogical and philosophical changes by social science academics working in pandemic conditions, it has been a longer than anticipated road to publication. Aside from normal publication challenges, the pandemic itself took its added toil on our authors who battled their own personal and work challenges to help bring this work to fruition. The result is a small but innovative anthology of pedagogical approaches to social science teaching under pandemic conditions. The individual works are a testament to academics and their commitment to their students and detail some of the challenges faced in the context of social science disciplines.

As Dean of the School of Social Sciences, I also have immense pride knowing that this book and publication is also in partnership with *Langaa Publishers*, a publishing house with a history of bringing African scholarship and the work of African scholars to the fore.

Vivian Ojong
Dean and Head of School of Social Sciences
University of KwaZulu-Natal
South Africa

The Pandemic and Social Science Approaches to Teaching and Learning

Maheshvari Naidu and Subashini Govender

University of KwaZulu-Natal

The global Coronavirus pandemic created seismic ruptures in what was before many routinised aspects of our daily lives and no less so in our work lives as academics, researchers and teachers. The world came to terms with what everyone was referring to as 'the so called new normal' [sic]. Even as that term was becoming sickeningly common and the word 'pandemic' became commonplace on everyone's lips (in the same way that the word 'tsunami' entered commonplace jargon in 2001), academics were obliged to confront how to engage with their students and how to have the students engage with their research.

The pandemic, thus, resulted in unprecedented and massive shifts in the social structuring of both work and personal lives. As countries around the globe initiated 'lockdown' procedures, to 'flatten the curve' and limit the transmission of the virus, governments, organisations, companies, institutions and the populace at large had to scramble to attempt to transform their lives within days (see Mahaye 2020; Mzileni 2020). Southern African institutions of higher education were of course not exempt from this change. To conform to government-led Covid-19 protocol, universities were compelled to completely shut down until further notice, students were hurried off from their residential accommodation at university to their hometowns and staff and students were asked to stay and work from home (Hendricks and Chirume 2020; SANews 2020).

The lockdown measures necessitated teaching and learning moving from the traditional face-to-face teaching approaches to online-based teaching, learning and engagement within a short period (Mahaye 2020 Mzileni 2000; Dipa 2020). The pandemic period presented exceptional challenges to all; both on personal levels as well as academic levels, as we moved to online and virtual platforms (Iwu 2022). Not only did teachers have to contend with navigating their students through a rapid transformation to online learning, but had to do so within the political asymmetries of a highly unequal society where teachers had to re-think teaching and learning while considering the deeply entrenched social inequalities faced by student populations (Mzileni

1

2020; Dipa 2020; Soudien 2020).

It was within this geo-political climate and context within which was embedded the further cosmological rupturing (al la Weick) where the world came to be segmented into 'pre-pandemic' or 'pre-covid' and 'post-pandemic' and 'post-covid. Resignation and resilience appeared to sit cheek to jowl in the context of what universities and academics had to do in tandem with the seemingly impossibility of what needed to be done. In many ways, arguably, resilience triumphed in many quarters. Resilience became not just a buzzword but took on mantra-like proportions. Resilience was also the adopted stance of institutions of higher learning which attempted to pivot and become agile in the manner in which teaching could be delivered and learning could be facilitated.

However, as universities strategised around the challenging enormity and the logistics of bringing online teaching to and into the homes of all students through the distribution of laptops and data (Cape Argus 2020; Universities South Africa 2020), the teaching staff were confronted with the pragmatics of negotiating the pedagogy of online teaching during crisis times. For academics at university, this move also underpinned other kinds of deeper epistemological shifts as they were compelled to rethink curriculum, assessment as well as their underlying teaching philosophies (see Govender and Rajkoomar 2021). This signified the dawn of a new era of pedagogical practices as new teaching approaches began to be utilised to create 'on-line communities of learning' on a previouly unprecedented scale. (Ravitch 2020). Since universities are (among other things) knowledge-producing institutions, the Covid-19 pandemic brought into question and up to the gaze how research could be conducted under the conditions of social distancing or (compelled) distance education.

Hedding et al. (2020:1) state that 'experiences of students and staff during the Covid-19 pandemic cannot be generalized'. Social science students and teachers/academics in the social sciences also experienced problems unique to their life situations and discipline (Iwu et al. 2022; Makwembere 2021). Social science teaching practices (pedagogy), in most Southern African universities traditionally focused on face-to-face lectures and tutorials, with supplementary course materials being posted on online platforms such as Moodle (in the context of the University of KwaZulu-Natal – UKZN). The social sciences at UKZN had thus engaged in blended learning prior to the Covid-19 pandemic (Khan et al. 2021; Iwu 2022). Blended learning was, thus, not a foreign concept to disciplines within the social sciences.

That said, as universities moved to general shutdown, teaching approaches shifted completely to online platforms. As mentioned, this move also symbolised attention to students' vulnerabilities and disadvantages, which

2

some scholars argued had hitherto received less attention than they deserved (see Mahaye 2020; Mzileni 2020). Such 'disadvantages', according to these scholars, included 'limited internet access, poor internet speed, and the high cost of internet' (Keržič et al. 2021: 5) as well as the realities of difficult living conditions, such as overcrowded homes, or homes that lacked basic amenities such as electricity or running water (Keržič et al. 2021). The challenge for social science and academics in social science was to navigate to online teaching while also addressing the broader social inequalities faced by their students.

This book responds to the undeniable shift and turning point in social science education and, as Soudien puts it, where students' identity and background impacts the learning process (Soudien 2020). This book is a modest attempt to engage with the responses from social science academics as they take into consideration the students' home environment and vulnerabilities. The book highlights their humanistic approach as they work with an understanding of the past traumas faced by students in conjunction with trauma related to Covid-19, and as they worked through an understanding of the local socio-cultural context in which students are embedded in, all of which impacts the learning process (Black et al. 2020). The chapters in this book showcase a humanistic and pragmatic pedagogy of response where pedagogy needed to transform to meet the needs of students. Such transformation included the 'co-creation of supporting learning environments' and introducing 'care' into pedagogy practices (Ravitch 2020; Bali 2020). Secondly, transforming to a more student-orientated teaching style opened new possibilities in curriculum development as the focus shifted from teacher-centred 'rote learning' methods to student-centred perspectives focusing on students' lived experiences, encouraging critical thinking and problem solving in their own social context (Govender and Rajkoomar 2021).

Thirdly, as pedagogy and curriculum transformed, so too did modes of assessments have to be rethought in line with new teaching practices (Allias and Marock 2020; Govender and Rajkoomar 2021). Social science assessments are predominately essay-based. During Covid-19, this posed a challenge to students and teachers alike. For instance, to write an essay, students need to engage in online and library research, read several texts on the topic and formulate ideas and an argument based on what they have read. This takes much time and effort. Since library facilities were indefinitely closed, students would have had to rely on online sources. However, this poses a problem for students living in areas in which electricity and internet services are weak and those who are unable to afford internet services (Hedding et al. 2020: 1). This opened new avenues for social sciences to rethink formative and summative assessments (Motala and Menon 2020). It provided an opportunity for social sciences lecturers to engage in creative assessment activities and tools that stimulate creative and critical thinking, while simultaneously being student centred (McInerney 2022).

Lastly, the research component of social sciences is also undergoing transformation. Traditionally, social science research focuses on face-to-face interviews, focus group interviews, survey questionnaires and methods of observation. These research methods involve contact with people, which was not possible during the Covid-19 pandemic (Hedding et al. 2020: 2). Since social science research is based on understanding the relationship between the individual/community/institution and wider society, it is important that this research continues during the pandemic in non-traditional but meaningful and scientifically valuable ways. This challenge opened new possibilities on how to engage with social science research without endangering the lives of both researcher and participants. It provided possibilities to creatively engage with new research methods and instruments for sourcing data and using technologies involved in engaging with participants, and opened up possibilities of doing research creatively.

These shifts in social science higher education pedagogy, curriculum, assessment and research mark a profound transformation from the traditional methods of teaching, learning and doing research to one that moved to actively engaging with southern African student needs, while creating innovative teaching and research methodologies embedded in local social contexts and knowledge. The book's purpose is to convey the challenges that Covid-19 presented to social science higher education as well as the numerous pedagogies that have emerged out of these challenges. This marks a turning point in social science education, which will have profound implications on the future spectrum of social science disciplines. Since this transformation is in a state of flux, it is imperative to capture these changes and new teaching techniques and practices in response to the Covid-19 pandemic that will undoubtedly continue to have long-term repercussions well after the pandemic has passed.

The book is located within the theme of teaching, learning and research in higher educational institutions in Southern Africa. Mgutshini et al. (2021) state that arguably fewer books are written, within a Southern African context, that examine the impact of Covid-19 on higher education institutions and how social science disciplines and teachers have contended with the impact of Covid-19. The book offers input through a social science prismatic lens as it combines broader factors such as the economic, political and socio-cultural aspects that impinge on students together with the everyday micro experiences that teachers and students go through as they adapt to using online learning platforms. Thus, the challenges of teaching during crisis are exposed in the chapters as well as the pedagogic shifts, utilised by the authors, captured. This pedagogic transformation includes the move to a more humanistic approach comprising aspects of care and a deeper understanding of the psycho-social issues students are faced with and attempting to co-create supportive learning environments (Ravitch 2020; Bali 2020), while using virtual technologies. According to Walwyn, the adjustment to online and virtual teaching modalities and blended learning approaches sees the promotion of 'open learning' (learning based on independent study instead of traditional classroom instruction) and 'open education' (increase in accessibility to online learning and training) (see Walwyn 2020:2). In addition, there is also a move towards and an opportunity for social justice educational outcomes. Arguably, institutions erected along business model designs have abandoned such values for an instrumental approach to higher education where graduates are educated with the unilineal dimensionality of contributing to the economy. Instead, a social justice approach advocates fair relationship between individual and society in which there is 'an equality in the distribution of wealth, opportunities, and privileges' (Walwyn 2020:2). These pedagogical shifts indicate a defining and historical moment in social science education that undoubtedly needs to be captured.

The current pandemic uniquely positions our contribution such that it captures the historical pedagogical shifts in social science in an unprecedented time. The book's main contribution is how teaching, learning and research are being conducted amongst social science academics and researchers in a global crisis. It offers insights on how social science academics are working under strenuous conditions to provide education to students by using online and virtual platforms to disseminate curricula, conduct assessments and to teach meaningfully. It also provides unique insights into the shift in pedagogy, curriculum development, assessments and research and the challenges and opportunities that come with these shifts.

Although there has been an increase in scholarship illustrative of the experiences of academics and the changes in teaching as a result of the Covid-19, much of this work, outlines experiences from the North (Murphy 2000; Morgan 2000), Europe (Willamson, Eynon and Potter 2000; Karalis and Raikou 2000) and Asia (Baloran 2000; Moorhouse 2000; Talidong and Toquero 2000). Thus, the experiences, situations and knowledge presented by African and South African academics are elided in the discourse and, in addition, much of the work published is in the fields of education and science. This offers an opportunity for local and global academics to understand the experiences of a South African university, specifically academics teaching the social sciences, and to learn from, implement and improve on pedagogies undertaken during a time of crisis.

This book specifically focuses on academics in the social science disciplines

5

within a South African higher education institutional context during and following the Covid-19 pandemic, and foregrounds new structural changes, student–teacher pedagogies and creative intellectual engagements.

References

Allais, S. and Marock, C. (2020) 'Educating for work in the time of Covid-19: Moving beyond simplistic ideas of supply and demand', *Southern African Review of Education*, Vol. 26. No. 1, pp. 62–79.

Bali, M. (2020) 'Pedagogy of Care: Covid-19 Edition', https://blog.mahabali.me/educational-technology-2/pedagogy-of-care-covid-19-edition/ (accessed 21 July 2020).

Baloran. T. E. (2020) 'Knowledge, attitudes, anxiety, and coping strategies of students during COVID-19 Pandemic', *Journal of Loss and Trauma*, DOI:10.1080/15325024.2020.1769300.

Black, S., Spreen, C. and Vally, S. (2020) 'Education, Covid-19 and care: Social inequality and social relations of value in South Africa and the United States', *Southern African Review of Education*, Vol. 26, No. 1, pp. 40–61.

Cape Argus (2020) This is how SA varsities are implementing online teaching amid Covid-19 lockdown', https://www.iol.co.za/capeargus/news/this-is-how-sa-varsities-are-implementing-online-teaching-amid-covid-19-lockdown-46930129 (accessed 21 July 2020).

Dipa, K. (2020) 'Covid-19 presents curricula crunch for SA's universities' Saturday Star 27 April 2020, https://www.iol.co.za/saturday-star/news/covid-19-presents-curricula-crunch-for-sas-universities-47191206 (accessed 21 July 2020).

Govender, R. and Rajkoomar, M. (2021) 'A multimodal model for learning, teaching and assessment in higher education', in T. Mgutshini, K. Oparinde and V. Govender (eds) *Covid-19: Interdisciplinary Explorations of Impacts on Higher Education*, Stellenbosch: *Africa Sun Media*.

Hedding, D. W., Greve, M., Breetzke, G. D., Nel, W. and Jansen van Vuuren, B. (2020) 'COVID-19 and the academe in South Africa: Not business as usual', *S Afr J Sci.*, Vol., 116, No. 7/8, https://doi.org/10.17159/sajs.2020/8298 (accessed 21 July 2020).

Hendricks, A. and Chirume, J. (2020) 'Covid-19: Universities across the country close', *Groundup* 17 March 2020, https://www.groundup.org.za/article/covid-19-universities-across-country-close/ (accessed 23 July 2020).

Iwu, C. G., Okeke-Uzodike, O. E., Anwana, E., Iwu, C. H. and Esambe, E. E. (2022) 'Experiences of academics working from home during COVID-19: A qualitative view from selected South African Universities', *Challenges*, pp. 13, 16, https://doi.org/10.3390/challe13010016 (accessed 23 August 2020).

Karalis, T. and Raikou, N. (2020). 'Teaching at the times of COVID-19: Inferences and implications for higher education pedagogy', *International Journal of Academic Research in Business and Social Sciences*, Vol. 10, No. 5, pp. 479–493.

Keržič, D., Alex J. K., Alvarado R. P. B., Bezerra, D. da S., Cheraghi, M., Dobrowolska B. *et al.* (2021) 'Academic student satisfaction and perceived performance in the elearning environment during the COVID-19 pandemic: Evidence across ten countries', *PLoS ONE*, Vol. 16, No. 10, e0258807, https://doi.org/10.1371/journal.pone.0258807 (accessed 30 August 2020).

Khan, N. B., Erasmus, T., Jali, N., Mthiyane, P. and Ronne, S. (2021) 'Is blended learning the way forward? Students' perceptions and attitudes at a South African university', *Afr J Health Professions Educ*, Vol. 13, No. 4, pp. 218–221, https://doi.org/10.7196/AJHPE.2021.v13i4.1424 (accessed 23 July 2020).

Mahaye, E. N. (2020) 'The Impact of COVID-19 Pandemic on Education: Navigating Forward the Pedagogy of Blended Learning', Department of Education KwaZulu-Natal.

Makwembere, S., Matarirano, O. and Jere, N. R. (2021) 'Lecturer autoethnographies of adjusting to online student interactions during COVID-19', *Research in Social Sciences and Technology*, Vol. 6, No. 2, pp. 148–168, https://doi.org/10.46303/ressat.2021.16 (accessed 30 July 2021).

McInerney P. A (2022) '… And then there was Covid!', *Afr J Health Professions Educ*, Vol. 14, No. 1, p. 2, https://doi.org/10.7196/AJHPE.2022.v14i1.1635 (accessed 23 July 2020).

Mgutshini, T., Oparinde, K. and Govender, V. (eds) Covid-19: Interdisciplinary Explorations of *Impacts on Higher Education*, Stellenbosch: *Africa Sun Media*.

Morgan, H. (2020) 'Best practices for implementing remote learning during a pandemic, the clearing house' *A Journal of Educational Strategies, Issues and Ideas*, Vol. 93, No. 3, pp. 135–141, DOI: 10.1080/00098655.2020.1751480 (accessed 23 July 2020).

Moorhouse, L. B. (2020) 'Adaptations to a face-to-face initial teacher education course "forced" online due to the COVID-19 pandemic', *Journal of Education for Teaching*, DOI: 10.1080/02607476.2020.1755205 (accessed 23 July 2020).

Motala, S. and Menon, K. (2020) 'In search of the "new normal": Reflections on teaching and learning during Covid-19 in a South African university', *Southern African Review of Education*, Vol. 26, No. 1, pp. 80–99.

Murphy, P. A. M. (2020) 'COVID-19 and emergency eLearning: Consequences of the securitization of higher education for post-pandemic pedagogy', *Contemporary Security Policy*, Vol. 41, No. 3, pp. 492–505, DOI: 10.1080/13523260.2020.1761749 (accessed 13 September 2020).

Mzileni, P. (2020) 'How Covid-19 will affect students', *Mail and Guardian* (23 April 2020) https://mg.co.za/education/2020-04-23-how-covid-19-will-affect-students/ (accessed 21 July 2020).

Ravitch, S. (2020) 'Pedagogy: Transforming Teaching & Learning during Coronavirus', *https://www.methodspace.com/flux-pedagogy-transforming-teaching-learning-during-coronavirus/* (accessed 21 July 2020).

SANews (2020) South African Government News Agency 'Task team to address Covid-19 response in higher education' 25 March 2020, https://www.sanews.gov.za/south-africa/task-team-address-covid-19-response-higher-education (accessed 23 July 2020).

Soudien, C. (2020) 'Systemic shock: How Covid-19 exposes our learning challenges in education', *Southern African Review of Education*, Vol. 26, No. 1, pp. 6–19.

Talidong, B. J. K. and Toquero, D. M. C. (2020): 'Philippine teachers' practices to deal with anxiety amid COVID-19', *Journal of Loss and Trauma*, DOI:10.1080/15325024.2020.1759225.

UKZNDABA Campus Electronic Newsletter (2020) 'Decolonising of the Curriculum Using Anthropology', http://ndabaonline.ukzn.ac.za/UkzndabaStory/Vol8Issue32/Decolonising%20of%20the%20Curriculum%20Using%20Anthropology (accessed 1 August 2020).

Universities South Africa (2020) 'Public universities have either embraced emergency teaching/learning, or are getting ready for the inevitable, in the COVID-19 era', https://www.usaf.ac.za/universities-coronavirus-covid-19-updates/ (accessed 23 July 2020).

Walwyn, D. R. (2020) 'Teaching on the edge of chaos: Report on "The future of universities in a post-COVID-19 world"', *S Afr J Sci*, Vol. 116, No. 7/8, https://doi.org/10.17159/sajs.2020/8404 (accessed 23 July 2020).

Williamson, B., Eynon, R. and Potter, J. (2020) 'Pandemic politics, pedagogies and practices: digital technologies and distance education during the coronavirus emergency', *Learning, Media and Technology*, Vol. 45, No. 2, pp. 107–114, DOI:10.1080/17439884.2020.1761641 (accessed 3 July 2020).

Chapter 1

Research, Supervision and Publishing in the Time of Pandemics: A South African Perspective

Goolam Vahed

University of KwaZulu-Natal

Introduction

The coronavirus pandemic currently sweeping the world has resulted in a South Africa-wide lockdown to slow down the spread of the disease. This has led to the cancellation of face-to-face classes at universities as well as academic conferences and graduation ceremonies, a halt to research and delays in publication. While universities are moving towards online teaching, research poses unique challenges for academics as well as postgraduate students being trained in research methods and/or undertaking research for their dissertations. This calls on us to re-think our research modules, our expectations of students and the kinds of research we conduct. How do we do research without everyday fieldwork? What will a new form of ethics mean? When allowed to do so, how do we conduct oral histories in communities affected by disasters and pandemics? How do we shield ourselves from pain and trauma? How do we construct safe environments for researchers as well as informants to tell their stories? Is it time for more research repositories and libraries to make their material available online? This chapter considers some of these questions and challenges.

The global coronavirus (Covid-19) pandemic that is sweeping grimly across the world is unprecedented. Other epidemics such as HIV/AIDS (Iliffe 2006) and Ebola (Richards 2016), were regionally confined and during these, and even the Spanish Flu outbreak of 1918, the world was never shut down to the extent that it has been in 2020 in terms of work, travel and movement. In an effort to slow the spread of the virus, South African President, Cyril Ramaphosa, declared a state of disaster on 15 March 2020. Professor Nana Poku, Vice-Chancellor and Principal of the University of KwaZulu-Natal (UKZN), issued a communiqué on 15 March 2020 announcing the suspension of the academic programme, cancellation of the graduation ceremony and prohibition of university-related international and non-essential domestic travel.

On 17 March 2020, Minister of Higher Education, Blade Nzimande, instructed universities to go into recess from 18 March until at least mid-April 2020. On 22 March 2020, President Ramaphosa announced a three-week nationwide lockdown with effect from midnight on 26 March 2020. With the exception of those involved in providing 'essential services', all South Africans were required to stay at home. This had a direct bearing on teaching and research. Minister Nzimande called on universities to make preparations to switch to online learning. UKZN put training programmes in place to assist academics to begin recording and loading their lectures onto virtual platforms. Lectures were to begin online from 1 June 2020. UKZN has five campuses, around 50,000 students (with roughly half living in the university's residences) and some 9,000 staff in total.

The sudden suspension of the academic programme raised many questions. Was the rush to online teaching a contingency measure or would it become a permanent feature of the tertiary landscape? What should students do? Throw in the towel? Take a year off? What happens to those who cannot complete their research because of restrictions? These are some of the difficult issues that administrators, academics, students and parents grappled with, as online learning is not the panacea that it is sometimes made out to be.

Indeed, some academics have warned of the impact of online teaching and learning on students and the transformation agenda in South Africa. As Baum and McPherson (2019: 235) state:

> Strong evidence indicates that students with weak academic backgrounds and other risk factors struggle most in fully online courses, creating larger socioeconomic gaps in outcomes than those in traditional classroom environments. The central problem appears to be the lack of adequate personal interaction between students and instructors, as well as among students. Hybrid learning models do not exhibit the same problems and there is potential for online learning to develop strategies for overcoming these difficulties. Meanwhile, narrowing gaps in educational opportunities and outcomes requires considerable skilled human interaction.

The shutting down of universities generated urgent discussion within the academic community on the impact of the pandemic on undergraduate and postgraduate programmes, as well as research by academic staff. The move to online learning presented staff and students with numerous challenges due to the fact that many students did not have sufficient data, laptops or even electricity. This was exacerbated by load shedding, which has been a feature of South African society since around 2008. Universities have attempted to address these issues through such measures as providing data bundle packages to students and staff, negotiating a 'zero-rated' status for UKZN's most used URLs with telecommunication companies and training staff to deliver online teaching material (through audio PowerPoints, for example). The efficacy of these measures is discussed below.

This chapter is not concerned with the efficacy of online teaching as such, but it examines some of these concerns with specific reference to my own research as a historian based at UKZN, and how the pandemic is affecting postgraduate students in the History Department, though the issues raised here apply to other disciplines as well, as do the consequences for staff, students and the university more generally. I am approaching this research as both an 'insider', meaning that this research is within my own work practice, and 'outsider', which allows for critical academic distance, and leave it to the reader to assess the advantages and disadvantages of my situatedness.

In terms of methodology, the chapter is based on the author's own experiences and self-reflection, known as 'autoethnography' in qualitative research methodology. While there is no precise definition of autoethnography, it does involve 'insider ethnography', in this case my being a member of the History Department which is the subject of this study. This mode of research values the researcher's relationship with others and involves relating the 'autobiographical and personal to the cultural, social, and political' (Ellis 2004: xix).

The Pandemic and UKZN's Mission

Goal 2 of UKZN's Strategic Plan 2017–2021, 'To achieve Excellence and High Impact in Research, Innovation and Entrepreneurship,' states that,

> … the goal is to build a research ethos which acknowledges the responsibility of academic staff to nurture their postgraduate students, and to build UKZN as a pre-eminent producer of new knowledge that is both local and global in context, and which defines UKZN as the Premier University of African Scholarship.

The key question is: How will the pandemic and associated measures impact on UKZN's mission of becoming a globally ranked university that both trains postgraduate students and produces quality research that responds to contemporary challenges?

As a preface to our discussion, it should be pointed out that more than half the students entering UKZN are from lower quintile schools and are generally underprepared for tertiary education. In a communiqué to staff, dated 17 October 2019, Professor Poku stated:

11

We are very proud to be the most transformed of the research-intensive universities in South Africa – with more than 58 percent of our new recruits this year coming from quintile 1-3 schools[1] Some of our most pressing challenges arise from the fact that UKZN is ill prepared (administratively, academically and infrastructurally) for supporting our rapid expansion of quintile 1–3 students and their transitional needs to higher education. This creates strains in everything from safe and secure student accommodation to teaching facilities and the university's academic reputation – particularly maintaining an elite research status as a university.

A substantial proportion of students who enrol at UKZN are African, from rural or peri-urban areas, and from a lower socio-economic background. As Jack (2019: 21) points out, high schools 'play a powerful role in shaping students' cultural competencies'. Furthermore, student success is 'shaped by their access to material resources – money – or lack thereof'. Many of our students are encumbered by race, class and gender disadvantages, as well as the poor quality of high school education, exacerbated by 'structural inequality' within universities whose policies further disadvantage them, as discussed later in this chapter. Also rarely emphasised is that most of these students are first-generation in that many of their parents have not been to high school, let alone university. Many consequently lack 'some of the knowledge, called cultural capital', which is a key factor for success at tertiary level. First-generation students are less prepared for tertiary education (Ward, Siegal and Davenport 2012: 5).

The South African government has expanded access to tertiary education as a means to achieve African economic mobility since the country remains one of the most unequal societies in the world more than a quarter of a century into the post-apartheid period. The emphasis on postgraduate studies is also intended to produce more Africans with doctoral degrees, an aim given added urgency by student protests since 2016 calling for the decolonisation of education. Blade Nzimande, Minister of Higher Education, Science and Innovation, bemoaned the scarcity of African professors at tertiary institutions, where two-thirds of professors are still white (Lekgotla 2017). While well intended, one has to question the wisdom of the government spending hundreds of millions of rands producing countless doctorates in disciplines like history and anthropology where few jobs are available. That, however, is another issue for another time.

It is against this background that this chapter examines the impact that the pandemic is likely to have on research undertaken by academics and graduate students.

12

The Impact of the Pandemic on Academics' Research

The pandemic has impacted on academic research in terms of completing current projects as well as getting research published. This has major implications because the role of academics has changed markedly at many institutions in the past two decades due to institutional changes. As Bullough observed in 2014, the new 'market driven and profoundly entrepreneurial' model of universities is 'characterised by an intensity of research that far exceeds past experience' (2014: 23). To take history at the UKZN Howard College campus as an example, the number of permanent staff has dropped from eight to three over the past decade, while the number of students has increased five-fold. This has meant a far greater teaching workload for academics. At the same time, academics are pressured to bring in external funding; each has to supervise a minimum of six masters/doctoral students at any given time; and professors are required to publish a minimum of 2.5 journal articles per annum. None of this is humanly possible if one aims for the highest quality.

The UKZN Strategic Plan does not define what a 'research-intensive' university is. John Taylor, an academic at the University of Liverpool, identified key features of research-intensive universities as including 'pure and applied research; research-led teaching; breadth of academic disciplines; high proportion of postgraduate research programmes; high levels of external income; and an international perspective' (Taylor 2006: 4). Research-intensive universities should place emphasis on 'discovery research', with 'the creation of new knowledge ... at the heart of the institution and provided the vital lifeblood that sustained all other activities and forms of scholarship' (Taylor 2006: 9). These institutions also carefully monitor the 'performance of individual departments and schools; indeed, the performance culture extended to the level of individual members of staff'. This information was publicly available and exerted peer pressure on under-performing academics (Taylor 2006: 18).

As defined by Taylor, there are certain contradictions in theory and practice between UKZN's desire to be a research-intensive institution and the actual situation. The emphasis on quantification detracts from quality. It is virtually impossible to consistently publish groundbreaking work if one is required, as in the case of professors at UKZN, to publish 2.5 journal articles per annum, given the extremely high workloads, the time that it takes to produce creative research and writing and long waiting times in high impact journals. When research is evaluated by universities, little cognisance is taken of citations; application of research to current social, economic and political problems, or even academic distinctions such as editorships. According to Rawat and

Meena,

> The emphasis on publishing has decreased the value of the resulting scholarship as scholars must spend time scrambling to publish whatever they can manage, rather than spend time developing significant research agenda. The pressure to publish-or-perish also detracts from the time and effort professors can devote to teaching undergraduate and post-graduates. The rewards for exceptional teaching rarely match the rewards for exceptional research, which encourages faculty to favor the latter whenever they conflict. This single-minded focus on the professor-as-researcher may cause faculty to neglect or be unable to perform some other responsibilities (2014: 87).

Due to the pressure to publish, 'the pace of publication accelerates, encouraging projects that don't require extensive, time-consuming inquiry and evidence gathering' (Bauerlein et al. 2010: 13). Around 90 per cent of journal articles are never cited and 50 per cent are not read at all (Bullough 2014: 21). Much of the research produced in the academy is 'redundant, inconsequential, and outright poor … filling countless pages in journals and monographs' (Bauerlein et al. 2010: 13).

Smyth (2017: 2) regards the quantification culture as 'carnage being done to universities around the world' who are 'driven by the mantra of the performativity agenda'. It is detrimental to the academic functioning of universities since academics are reluctant to get involved in things like committee work and reviewing student proposals, because it takes away time from research. This audit culture has also led to the spawning of what are known as 'predatory' journals as academics, desperate to publish, find unethical ways of doing so. The targets set for academics are motivated by finance; each university in South Africa is given a block grant by the Department of Higher Education and Training for publications by staff members. This grant is critical to universities' sustaining themselves financially.

'Audit-induced competition'; 'command and control' managerialism; setting and relating 'grant income targets' for academics to performance management assessment; the fact that 'the work is simply never able to be finished; the goalposts are continually moved by management, so that faculty are never allowed to arrive at a definitive end to their work'; and casting academic work as not being mainly about the 'production and dissemination of knowledge', but about 'ensuring institutional survival and international economic competiveness … maximizing "profits" for the university' are leading to uncertainty and anxiety among academics (Smyth 2012: 9).

In sum, UKZN aspires to be the 'premier' university of African scholarship, but the model on which it is based detracts from the quality of research. Notwithstanding this criticism, the Covid-19 pandemic will have serious repercussions for this model of the South African university as academics are not able to carry out certain kinds of research, while publication of completed work is being delayed. For example, I was counting on a particular journal article to meet my performance management targets for 2020. The article has been peer-reviewed, revisions completed and the final version submitted to the journal. The editorial assistant advised on 16 June 2020: 'Thanks for getting this back so quickly. I've sent it through for production ... you should receive proofs sometime soon – although there is a considerable backlog because of the lockdown.' As pointed out, it seemed unlikely that the article would be published that year, which would have implications for my performance management rating.

A more serious problem is that of a full-length manuscript that a colleague and I submitted to a publisher in the first week of January 2020. The manuscript received positive reviews and we were busy revising it when we received the following 'bombshell' email from the publisher on 30 April 2020:

> While Press staff are thankfully all still in good health, the Press itself has taken rather a knock and we've had to reconsider our plans for the year. As you're probably aware, the global restrictions put in place to help stem the spread of SARS CoV-2, caused a drastic drop in book sales worldwide. ... Press depends on sales income to cover its operational costs (which include book production costs) and, even under normal circumstances, works on a very tight budget. Given the sharp drop in income occasioned by Covid-19-related restrictions and the uncertainty about when we will recover to a better position, we have decided to halt all new book production as well as the consideration of new manuscripts for the time being. We will review our situation in September. Regrettably, this means that we are therefore unable to further consider or put into production your manuscript you submitted earlier this year. We were very keen on the manuscript and regret having to let it go, but we are aware that it is time sensitive and therefore would understand if you sought and accepted other publishing offers. All is not doom and gloom though, as we will use this time to investigate a coherent e-publishing strategy, which we believe will strengthen our position.

We submitted the manuscript to another publisher and at the time of writing (September 2020), had received two positive reviews and notification that if the suggestions were addressed by November 2020, we could expect publication in November 2021, a year later than we had anticipated. November 2020 marks 160 years since the arrival of the first indentured migrants to Natal and it was our hope to have the book ready in time for this landmark occasion.

Contact with another publisher for a different project yielded the following reply on 15 June 2020: 'The book industry is down by 50% at the moment so we are having to think things through much more carefully going forward. Please be patient.'

On the one hand, with people stuck at home, this period should have been an opportunity for book sales. Mutinational companies like Amazon have benefited, as people confined at home have been searching for high quality reading material, not only for learning, teaching and research, but also for pleasure. Independent booksellers like Ike's in Durban and Clarke's in Cape Town, as well as Exclusive Books, on the other hand, were hard hit due to the shutdown of bookstores which eliminated 'foot traffic'. Academic publishers work on fine margins and their attitude appears to be one of wait-and-see as the publishing landscape is uncertain. Some major publishers, like Oxford University Press and Cambridge University Press, responded by making some resources available at no cost, but this is not sustainable in the long term.

Furthermore, academic conferences where these booksellers usually display and sell their books, such as the South African Historical Conference and the African Studies Association Conferences in the USA, UK and Europe, have been cancelled. As the email from the publisher with whom we were working shows, publishers are exploring the ebook option with greater urgency and it remains to be seen what the long-term consequences will be for the publishing industry.

How soon academics resolve the twin problems of completing current research as well as finding suitable outlets for completed research will depend to a large extent on how soon 'normalcy' returns. I am currently doing research on a project on a soccer club that is heavily based on oral interviews. Thirty interviews were planned and nine were completed at the time of the lockdown. The remaining interviews were to be completed by June 2020. This project has been delayed and I am concerned, not only because the research schedule has been disrupted, but that many of those whom I have to interview are in their late seventies and early eighties and if I am unable to interview them, an important collective memory on sport and the city of Durban will be lost. For example, I had set a date to interview Baboo Ebrahim, who was the team's first goalkeeper and represented the South African cricket team in one match, but this interview was postponed as he had to go out of town. Before we could reschedule the interview, Baboo Ebrahim contracted the coronavirus and passed away in July 2020 after a lengthy stay in hospital (see Daily News 21 July 2020).

Given the age profile and socio-economic background of the subjects of this study, Zoom/Skype interviews are rarely an option. In any event I have found that telephonic interviews are not as beneficial and valuable as face-to-face ones. Zoom is not a magic solution because there is sometimes a break in transmission, and words are lost. It is also hard to have follow-up questions and the flow of conversation is often interrupted. Personal contact and visual communication are important in the research process. The location where the interview takes place also provides visual cues. Nothing can beat talking to a real-life person.

The repercussions from the pandemic will be a blow to universities that base their reputation and financial well-being on funding generated from publishing. It remains to be seen what the exact consequences will be but, for now, it is clear that many universities abroad who are dependent on foreign students and student fees will be forced to shut down. The situation is marginally different in South Africa where the government provides subsidies to the sector, because of the large number of African students. While universities are unlikely to shut down, they will have to cut costs and this will likely include staff cuts as well as fewer services for students. Already, academic quality has been compromised by the practice of employing contract staff, who are mainly doctoral students, in place of permanent staff as a cost-cutting exercise.

This further loss of specialist skills and knowledge will impact on the university's ability to meet the country's social, environmental and economic challenges, as well as the needs of students. Non-employment of contract staff, who do considerable face-to-face teaching and grading of work, will increase the workload of permanent staff. This will reduce the time academics have to spend on research. It is also likely that university management, and maybe even the government, will reduce the financial incentive given to staff for publishing. As it is, academics receive, in real terms, considerably less that they received around fifteen years ago due to the fact that the incentive has been reduced, a fact compounded by the depreciation of the South African rand and inflation. In a context where the university does not provide research funding to academic staff, this will further impede staff research. It is unclear when the vicious cycle will end.

In summary, research done by academics faces a triple challenge: the difficulty of completing research, getting research published and cuts in future resources for research.

On the flip side, the short-term pause in research may have some benefits. As Gina Kolata (2017) has warned, many academics 'have become eager participants in what experts call academic fraud that wastes taxpayer money, chips away at scientific credibility, and muddies important research'. Perhaps this is a time for academics, administrators and bureaucrats to return to a consideration of why we are doing research and what we want to gain from it. The nett result may be research that is quantitatively reduced but qualitatively superior.

The Covid-19 pandemic is also having serious repercussions for postgraduate students.

Teaching and Supervision

In light of the state of disaster declared by President Ramaphosa, UKZN's School of Social Sciences (SoSS) Board resolved on 20 March 2020 to adopt regulations with regard to postgraduate research that were originally fashioned by the School of Education and adopted by Deans at College level. According to the document, although the university was in recess for undergraduate students, postgraduate supervision was to continue via modalities such as Zoom, which was supported by the university, or platforms like Skype/FaceTime/WhatsApp, which were not supported by the university. While face-to-face contact was prohibited, academics were instructed to 'maintain continuity without compromising the quality of the degree offerings'. These stipulations posed an immediate challenge for those doing fieldwork. The document advised:

> Fieldwork. This elicited major discussion regarding issues around not impacting on through-put as well as not impacting on quality of social science study if students opted to change methodology – i.e. much depends on the nature of methodological choices – mode must not include any contact/face to face data collection. To consider creative means that do not compromise integrity of study: Surveys – online/Questionnaires – online; Interviews – telephonically; Focus group interview – Skype, Zoom or postpone; Participant observation – postpone/ Observations – postpone; Change methodology – from fieldwork to systematic review or use of secondary data sources – NOTE that this will require new ethical clearance, although this will be expedited if fully Desktop.

The dilemmas posed by the coronavirus are evident. The directive prohibited face-to-face data collection but did not want this to affect either throughput or quality. Researchers were further handicapped because archives, libraries and documentation centres that house newspapers and manuscripts were closed as a result of the national lockdown regulations. While coursework honours and masters' courses can be taught online, there is a great challenge for those doing full research masters and doctoral dissertations that involve face-to-face interviews and ethnography, as well as archival research.

Our postgraduate courses teach students some of the basic historical methods which they are able to apply in the course of their research for their dissertations, and these theoretical and practical research skills can be transferred to other professional settings. Amongst the skills taught are using the archives wherein they learn to locate, study and analyse historical documents. Also crucial to the historical process are visual materials like photographs, the setting in which people live, and analysing and interpreting historical sources, searching past newspapers. These are all problematic at the present time. Other skills can be taught, such as referencing one's research appropriately (such as Chicago/Harvard styles), managing citations (EndNote/Zotero); thinking critically, and preparing questionnaires (how to design questions; limiting questions, asking broader questions; not making prior assumptions when asking questions). Students also learn the ways to record interviews and transcribe them.

These issues are examined in relation to some of the students currently being supervised in history.

Student One

The student is completing a PhD on the Group Areas Act and forced removals. The student had intended to submit his dissertation by the end of 2020. However, the pandemic presented two problems – the candidate is currently unable to complete follow-up oral interviews or consult court records and newspapers for an important chapter. As Roy (2020) points out, in the process of research, 'the ethnographer may want to return to the field, the historian to the archive, the chemist to the lab, or the literature scholar to a rare manuscript in a library, to see if it indeed can be elaborated upon. All of these are impossible longings for the researcher during the pandemic.'

This doctoral student is currently completing his revisions and editing the other chapters, in the hope that restrictions will be lifted soon and that he will be allowed to complete the remaining research. If this is not possible, the student will likely have to omit this chapter, which would be unfortunate. As with other students, internet access is a huge problem. For example, when I requested student one to send me his completed chapters, he wrote back:

From: …@ukzn.ac.za>
Sent: Sunday, 21 June 2020 12:56
To: Goolam Vahed <VAHEDG@ukzn.ac.za>
Subject: Re: RE:

Alright Prof I finished them already. will send tomorrow. I'm home in the rural areas. network is a problem on this side.

Student Two

The second student is doing research on farmworkers. His topic is: 'In their own words: The untold story of marginalized farm workers in KwaZulu-Natal, 1960s-2000s'. This dissertation focuses on the lives of farmworkers in the Umvoti region of KwaZulu-Natal where the student grew up. In the student's words, 'their struggles have been marginalized in the historiography and this dissertation will help to give voice to them, but beyond that contribute to the emerging literature on farmworkers and their place in the political economy of South Africa.' Archival research was to be carried out at the Alan Paton Centre and Struggle Archives on UKZN's Pietermaritzburg campus, as well as the Pietermaritzburg Archives Repository. More importantly, the candidate was to conduct twenty interviews with farmworkers (current and retired) to gain insight into their past and present experiences. The candidate has completed his proposal, some archival work and five interviews. He is busy transcribing those interviews. Interviews cannot be conducted with farmworkers who mostly live in rural areas without access to Wi-Fi and internet to do interviews via Zoom or Skype.

Student Three

This student is focusing on Group Areas removals in Pietermaritzburg. The dissertation is titled, 'Community, Identity, and Memory: Group Areas and the forced relocation of "Coloureds" to Woodlands, Pietermaritzburg, 1960-1990'. The student is investigating the impact of the Group Areas Act of 1950 in the making of Pietermaritzburg, with particular reference to the coloured community. This study will examine the process of removals, resistance and the impact this had on the residents who were relocated. It will examine the making of community in the new townships and the trauma that the coloured community suffered. The study is based on archival research at the Alan Paton Archives, the Natal Archives Repository and the Bessie Head Library, all in Pietermaritzburg, as well as fifteen interviews with community leaders, religious figures and ordinary residents. The student has completed five interviews and is busy transcribing these and writing up background chapters on the basis of available research. Interviews can probably be conducted with a few individuals via Zoom or Skype but others do not have access to the internet and Wi-Fi. Archival research cannot be concluded at the present time.

Student Four

He is researching for a master's dissertation on an 'Intellectual biography of an African Philosopher'. The dissertation seeks to understand why so few universities in the world offer courses on African Philosophy which, as a discipline, is more than a century old and there is no shortage of teaching materials. It aims to examine the history, growth, importance and relevance of African Philosophy through a study of the life and work of philosopher Jonathan Okeke Chimakonam. It is located in the context of calls to decolonise education. The thesis was to be based on an interview with the professor and his family and friends, and an analysis of his works. Skype or Zoom can be used to conduct interviews, while 'desktop research' is involved in the analysis of the philosopher's works.

While the student can proceed with the research once ethical clearance has been granted, he faces other challenges. The first concerns data and access to Wi-Fi. The university promised data to all students but at the time of writing (18 June 2020) many students had not received it even though classes had begun. Some classes have already been suspended. Thus, when preparing the proposal, this student wrote to me:

> **From:** …
> **Sent:** Thursday, 02 April 2020 19:04
> **To:** Goolam Vahed <VAHEDG@ukzn.ac.za>
> **Subject: Re:** Attachment
> Hi, I apologize for my late response. Due to the lockdown I have severely limited access to the internet. I am not sure what and how to move henceforth.
> Regards
> …

What could I say? I replied on the same day: 'We can take it forward when you have access to internet, until then I am not sure what you can do.'

The proposal was eventually completed in June 2020 and, as is standard practice, students usually present the proposal to the school at which there is robust questioning. The proposal includes such things as the scope of the study, the literature review, theoretical framework, methodology, chapter breakdown and time framework. The format for the presentation and defence of research proposals has changed. According to the Covid-19 Higher Degrees protocol adopted on 1 April 2020 students are to adopt the following procedure until further notice:

1. Proposals (+ the student's PowerPoint presentations slides) will be emailed as usual (by the supervisor) to the Cluster Higher Degrees Committee coordinators/chairs (within submission deadline).
2. Our cluster defence presentations are to be driven by round robin using emailing (we will not have Zoom virtual presentations at this stage because of connectivity problems for students). Where possible, AUDIO (not video) should be added to the PPT presentation so that staff will get a chance to hear the students' presentation. This also gives the students the chance to practise their presentations.
3. There must be TWO reviewers (assigned by the coordinator/chair) for all Masters and PhD proposals.
4. Once the reviewer reports are in, these will be circulated together with the proposal and PPT slides to all staff. Staff will use these to craft their own responses to the proposal. A tight deadline will be given for this because it adds a layer of review that was not accounted for when the Committee schedule was designed earlier in the year.
5. At the end of each month, staff feedback will be facilitated in a short Zoom meeting that will be held to collectively decide on the fate of the proposal(s). This is to ensure transparency and collective decision making, and to ensure that the 'meeting' aspect of the Committee takes place.
6. After each Zoom meeting the committees' comments + the two reviewers' reports for each Masters and PhD student will be emailed to the relevant supervisor so that he/she can work with his/her student to revise the proposal as required before submission to higher degrees.

In addition to these constraints, we need to factor in the need for an enabling environment. Students were told to leave their residences and history students will not be amongst those prioritised when students return to campus. Many live in informal settlements where electricity and internet connectivity are perennial challenges.

Implications for Training Future Historians

The pandemic has 'thrown into question basic assumptions about how we do what we do and how we know what we know' (DeHart 2020). As is evident from these examples, postgraduate students currently in our programme are faced with several challenges. So many taken for granted aspects of postgraduate study have been disrupted – access to materials, proposal defence, robust discussion, research fieldwork, and so on. History as a discipline has specific ways of carrying out research, an important aspect of which is archival research which distinguishes it from other disciplines. As Souradeep Roy (2020) reflected:

Historians specialising in specific fields and time-periods take up research questions which require them to visit specific libraries (or archives). Here they find either their friends and/or foes ... the librarians and staff. It is difficult to explain the thrill of seeing files numbered DL/145/1556 open up for you, as if it holds some kind of secret that would answer a troubling question in the head. ... It leads to more files, more questions. ... What the pandemic has done is stop this quest in some ways.

A major part of the problem for historians doing research is that archival records in most countries are not digitised. Digitisation is important to allow access to researchers but also to ensure that valuable records are not lost as a result of fading or disintegration through repeated handling. Documents are unlikely to be digitised in the near future because of the volume of documents (automatic feeders cannot work with bound volumes of brittle documents), the costs involved and because archives are territorial over their holdings. Digitising is not a magic wand since technology can be corrupted and it changes over time (see Thompson 2017), but in view of the pandemic, a start should be made somewhere.

Oral history has also been increasingly utilised by historians. As Gunn and Faire (2012: 2) point out, 'what has been significant about the various "turns" affecting the human sciences over the last three decades – linguistic, spatial, material, and so on – has been the extent to which they left the basic procedures of history intact'. Historians are increasingly utilising methodologies like life histories based on oral history, thus overlapping with those utilised in the social sciences.

The problem for our postgraduate students is that at the time of writing we have limited knowledge of the virus' life-span. The policy of the South African government and that of UKZN will depend on the trajectory of the virus or new knowledge about its behaviour. While many sectors of the economy have been opened, in his address to the nation on 17 June 2020, President Cyril Ramaphosa warned, 'even after 100 days, we are still near the beginning of this epidemic and it will remain with us for many more months, possibly years. The task of dealing with the coronavirus pandemic is like running a marathon race and not a sprint, and we have therefore had to shape our response according to that reality'. The problem is that running a marathon takes preparation and one knows the route. But the corona marathon has afforded us little time to prepare, the route is unmarked and the finishing line is undetermined.

Minister Nzimande announced on 23 May 2020, that when South Africa moved to level three of the lockdown on 1 June 2020, a maximum of a third (two-thirds at level 2 and 100 per cent at level 1) of students were to be allowed back on campus. Professor Poku issued a *communiqué* on 19 June 2020 that in line with government policy, priority would be given to final year students in clinical training and those who required access to laboratory equipment. With regard to postgraduate students, the communiqué stated that it would only include 'students who require access to laboratory equipment'.

President Ramaphosa announced on 16 September 2020 that the country had 'withstood' the coronavirus pandemic and would move to level 1 from midnight on Sunday 20 September 2020. While, in theory, this meant that all students could return to campus, as per an email from Professor S.P. Songca, Deputy Vice-Chancellor: Teaching and Learning, UKZN, dated 16 September 2020, 'Academics will once again upload learning materials on Moodle and students will engage in self-directed learning according to the blended learning and flipped classroom pedagogies.' Online learning is to continue through the second semester which runs from 21 September to 18 December 2020.

It is difficult to predict what the eventual social and economic consequences of the pandemic will be and how this will affect the communities/individuals being studied. This is particularly the case with the rural and urban poor who may be more vulnerable than middle-class South Africans because of age or because they are immuno-compromised. The projects discussed here depend heavily on close interaction and face-to-face interviews and there is a danger that the students may themselves be a vector for the virus and constitute a danger to vulnerable communities (Wood, Rogers, Sivaramakrishnan and Almeling 2020). Thus, even when policy makes field research possible, the wellbeing of the persons being studied must be taken into account.

Historians doing fieldwork, especially conducting interviews, have to build trust, which is achieved through close interaction and the development of relationships. As DeHart warns,

> Digital media of the kind to which we've quickly turned in this crisis offers a useful communicative tool for conducting interviews or

meetings; however, it is neither universally available nor reliable for all researchers and their subjects. What's more, digital media erases from view the social context of those conversations, at best complementing rather than substituting in-person exchanges (DeHart 2020).

Another aspect of the academic process affected by the pandemic is the cancellation of conferences. Conferences are important for academics to build networks that will lead to invitations to other conferences, to contribute to edited books and specials issues of journals, to participate in large funding projects, and so on. They are also important opportunities for postgraduate students to develop their presentation skills, learn from presentations by experienced academics, improve their expertise in a particular field and, perhaps, secure interviews for academic positions. In these Covid times, many institutions and conference organisers have been forced to resort to Zoom webinars, which can be accessed from virtually anywhere in the world. Until around 2014, the History Department at UKZN ran a very successful weekly seminar. This stopped once most of the senior academics took up positions at other institutions. One of our former colleagues, Julie Parle, initiated the resuscitation of the seminar on a monthly basis from June 2020. It has drawn together historians from different parts of the country. We are also able to connect with similar seminars at institutions in various part of the world. While we would welcome a return to large real-life conferences, it is hoped that access to these seminars will continue as it will supplement conferences.

Conclusion

The Covid-19 pandemic has impacted on the tertiary sector in general and especially teaching and research in fundamental ways. If there are job cuts and fewer academics in each discipline, it will impact on teaching and intellectual life. History, for example, used to run a vibrant weekly seminar programme and produced a journal. Both activities have been shed as a result of the departure of academics. Research will also be affected. Technology has many uses but is unlikely to be the panacea for academic teaching and research in the South African context. Bret Stephens of The New York Times (6 November 2018) wrote that the reason why 'technology so often disappoints and betrays us is that it promises to make easy things that, by their intrinsic nature, have to be hard'. Effective teaching, whether online or in traditional settings, is hard (in Baum and McPherson 2019: 235).

Archival and in-person field research (oral interviews) is crucial for historians. Research via Zoom may work in some settings but faces many constraints in the South African context where the subjects of study are often working class or lack technology. Historians in training cannot complete viable projects through desktop research or online questionnaires, and, in any event, for many of our students the home is not the ideal place to write.

For the foreseeable future then, the postgraduate programme in history faces serious logistical and ethical challenges in providing adequate training. In the case of my research as well as that of our postgraduate students, we are faced with critical questions in the coming months:

> These include not just how we do research and the ethical questions of continuing to research, even in novel ways, during Covid, but also whether we continue to do research, the complications of postponement and restarting research, and the implications of cancellation. There may be situations in which the most ethical response is to weigh the value of research itself against the dangers, rather than merely seeking ways to continue while minimizing danger. Alternatively, putting research on hold raises questions about responsibility to participants, time-sensitive data, and unfinished projects (Carayannis and Bolin 2020).

As I complete this chapter, there are more questions than answers as far as postgraduate studies are concerned. At this stage (September 2020), the restriction on face-to-face research remains in place. When will contact interviews be permitted? Even if permitted by the university, will individuals who are to be interviewed be willing to do so? Will organisations provide gatekeepers' letters? There are no definite answers to these questions at this stage. It will depend entirely on the course of the pandemic and people's attitudes towards it.

The pandemic is clearly posing serious challenges to postgraduate students attempting to complete their dissertations, an undertaking that is so crucial for training future historians. The uncertainty around the virus means uncertainty for students who are not sure whether and how they will complete their projects or whether it will be necessary to find projects that will not require fieldwork or even archival work.

The irony is that this is happening in a world where original research is more important than ever as we seek to navigate a path through incredible uncertainty and fear.

References

Bauerlein, M., Gad-el-Hak, M., Grody, W. McKelvey, B. and Trimble, S. W. (2010) 'We must stop the avalanche of low-quality research', *The Chronicle of Higher Education*, 13 June, https://www.chronicle.com/article/We-Must-Stop-the-Avalanche-of/65890 (accessed 17 June 2020).

Baum, S. and McPherson, M. (2019) 'The Human Factor: The Promise & Limits of Online Education', *Dædalus, the Journal of the American Academy of Arts & Sciences*, pp. 235–254.

Bullough, R. V. (2014) 'Higher education and the neoliberal threat. Place, fast time and identity', *Journal of Thought*, pp.13–32.

Carayannis, T. and Bolin, A. (2020) 'Research in Insecure Times and Places: Ethics of Social Research for Emerging Ecologies of Insecurity, Social Science Research Council, 21 May, https://items.ssrc.org/covid-19-and-the-social-sciences/social-research-and-insecurity/research-in-insecure-times-and-places-ethics-of-social-research-for-emerging-ecologies-of-insecurity/ (accessed 16 June 2020).

DeHart, M. (2020) 'Thinking Ethnographically in Pandemic Times', Social Science Research Council, 21 May, https://items.ssrc.org/covid-19-and-the-social-sciences/social-research-and-insecurity/thinking-ethnographically-in-pandemic-times/ (accessed 16 June 2020).

Ellis, C. (2004) *The Ethnographic I: A Methodological Novel about Autoethnography*. Walnut Creek: AltaMira Press.

Gunn, S. and Faire, L. (2012) 'Introduction: Why Bother with Method?', in S. Gunn and L. Faire (eds) *Research Methods for History, Edinburgh: Edinburgh University Press*, pp. 1–12.

Iliffe, J. (2006) *The African Aids Epidemic: A History, Athens*, OH: Ohio University Press.

Jack, A. A. (2019) *The Privileged Poor: How Elite Colleges Are Failing Disadvantaged Students*, Cambridge, Massachusetts: Harvard University Press.

Kolata, G. (2017) 'Many Academics are eager to publish in worthless journals', *New York Times*, 30 October, https://www.nytimes.com/2017/10/30/science/predatory-journals-academics.html (accessed 18 September 2020).

Lekgotla, N. (2017) 'Why are there so few black professors?', *Mail & Guardian*, 15 June, https://mg.co.za/article/2017-06-15-00-why-are-there-so-few-black-professors/ (accessed 18 June 2020).

Rawat, S. and Meena, S. (2014) 'Publish or perish: Where are we heading?', *Journal of Research and Medical Sciences*, Vol. 19, No. 2, pp. 87–89.

Richards, P. (2016) *Ebola. How a People's Science Helped End an Epidemic*, London: Zed Books.

Roy, S. (2020) 'Why the pandemic will lead to a drop in publishing of research: W(riting) FH does not work', *Scroll.in*, 17 September, https://scroll.in/article/973356/why-the-pandemic-will-lead-to-a-drop-in-publishing-of-research-w-riting-fh-does-not-work (accessed 18 September 2020).

Smyth, J. (2017) *The Toxic University. Zombie Leadership*, Academic Rock Stars and Neoliberal Ideology, London: Palgrave Macmillan.

Thompson, S. (2017) 'Why don't archivists digitize everything?', Peel Art Gallery Museum and Archives (PAMA), 31 May, https://peelarchivesblog.com/2017/05/31/why-dont-archivists-digitize-everything/ (accessed 21 June 2020).

Taylor, J. (2006) 'Managing the unmanageable: The management of research in research-intensive universities', *Higher Education Management and Policy*, Vol. 18, No. 2, pp. 1–25.

University of KwaZulu-Natal (2016) *University of KwaZulu-Natal (UKZN) Strategic Plan 2017–2021*, https://strategicplan17-21.ukzn.ac.za/ (accessed 14 June 2020).

Ward, L., Siegal, M. J. and Davenport, Z. (2012) *First-Generation College Students: Understanding and Improving the Experience from Recruitment to Commencement*, San Fransisco: Jossey-Bass.

Wood, E. J., Rogers, D., Sivaramakrishnan, K. and lmeling, R. (2020) 'Resuming Field Research in Pandemic Times', Social Science Research Council, 21 May, https://items.ssrc.org/covid-19-and-the-social-sciences/social-research-and-insecurity/resuming-field-research-in-pandemic-times/ (accessed 16 June 2020).

Endnotes

1 Schools in South Africa are classified according to five quintiles (1-5), with quintile one being situated in the poorest socio-economic areas with fewest resources. Many studies show that learners from these schools have consistently lower achievement at all cognitive levels.

Chapter 2

New Spaces of Engagement in Higher Education: An Exploration of the Use of WhatsApp Groups by Staff and Students in the School of Social Sciences during the Covid-19 Pandemic

Mark Rieker

University of KwaZulu-Natal

Introduction

The World Health Organisation officially recognised the spread of the Covid-19 virus as a pandemic on 11 March 2020. Soon thereafter, on 15 March 2020, the South African government invoked the Disaster Management Act (No. 57 of 2002) and declared a national state of disaster. Eight days later the president of South Africa announced a nationwide lockdown to begin on 27 March 2020. Under the lockdown, severe restrictions were put in place to limit the spread of the virus. South Africa, along with most other countries in the world, was plunged into an unprecedented situation of uncertainty with all sectors of the country having to respond drastically to curb the spread of the virus. Economic, social and cultural activities which involved human interaction were severely limited to ensure social distancing.

The education sector was particularly affected with schools closing and a shift from a traditional, classroom-based model to remote, online forms of teaching and learning. The higher education sector saw an exodus of students and staff from campuses and residences. Conventional learning spaces moved from the physical to the virtual with staff and students alike having to quickly and without sufficient preparation make use of online platforms, devices and applications to continue the curriculum. A period of adjustment, uncertainty and innovation followed. The Covid-19 pandemic will provide a rich and varied basis for scholarship and research for years to come. Social science disciplines such as anthropology, economics, sociology, political science, psychology and education will be able to apply theoretical and conceptual frameworks to explore and explain the social effects of the pandemic. There is also an opportunity to take stock of and reflect upon accepted normative approaches to pedagogy and the role of technology in the higher education sector.

This chapter will examine a particular aspect of the higher education sector's response to the national lockdown by focusing on the idea of virtual spaces of learning and engagement. Social distancing, as a means to limit the spread of the virus, can be construed as simply a change of social spatial arrangements: de-emphasising the physical and promoting the virtual. These virtual spaces are many and varied. The emphasis of the chapter will be on a particular form of virtual space – the WhatsApp group. The lockdown has resulted in an increased use of, and reliance on, WhatsApp groups by staff and students at the University of KwaZulu-Natal. These groups replaced traditional forms of interaction and became primary sites of information, knowledge and resource sharing. These groups are of various sizes, are both formal and informal, are populated by staff, students or a mixture of both and are created to serve assorted functions. Although WhatsApp is not an official method of teaching and learning, its use serves to buttress the change to and use of non-traditional methods of teaching and learning in a time of uncertainty and flux in educational praxis.

Soon after the national lockdown, the University of KwaZulu-Natal in South Africa put in place interim policies to manage its institutional response. The School of Social Sciences assembled an Online Learning Task Team to spearhead the school's response to online learning. As part of its mandate, the task team surveyed staff and students about various aspects of the shift to online teaching and learning. This survey will serve as a basis for a discussion of virtual spaces such as WhatsApp groups as new sites of engagement. The research problem is concerned within the intersection of traditional and virtual pedagogies in an environment of incremental change towards adoption of information and communication technologies (ICTs) and the unexpected adoption of a full online model of teaching and learning necessitated by the Covid-19 pandemic. The specific focus is on the use of WhatsApp groups as a model of organic and innovative pedagogical support outside of normative pedagogical frameworks. The exploration and analysis are framed in the context of social practice theory and specifically adopt Shove et al.'s (2012) Three Element Model of social practice. The use of social practice theory is appropriate here as the unit of analysis is not the content of the WhatsApp groups themselves, but rather the reported reflections on these groups by staff and students. This model allows an understanding of the elements of social practice at play when using the groups for educational purposes.

Shifting Spaces of Teaching, Learning and Engagement

The traditional model of higher education involved the 'sage on a stage' approach. Learners would congregate in a physical space such as a classroom or lecture hall and listen to the lecturer expound on a subject. Such spaces were characterised by an emphasis on the delivery of instruction and were 'static, stable and location specific' (Czerniewicz and Brown 2010: 149). Rovai and Jordan (2004) argue that the early transformation of higher education involved, in part, a shift from this emphasis on instruction to an emphasis on the production of learning. This new emphasis embraced innovation in the higher education sector and, with it, new forms and modes of teaching, which could more effectively produce enhanced learning outcomes.

In the 1990s, with the use of the internet and electronic forms of communication becoming widespread, the potential of these nascent technologies for enhancing learning began to be explored. In 1994, Davis and Botkin speculated that the 'schoolhouse of the future, [...] may be neither school nor house' (Davis and Botkin: 23). This foreshadowed the evolution of the educational enterprise from traditional to new forms of teaching, learning and engagement.

Electronic learning (or elearning), is defined by the Organisation for Co-operation and Development (OECD) as 'the use of information and communications technology (ICT) to enhance and/or support learning' (ICT 2005: 2). Technologies such as the internet and email created new approaches to teaching and learning but they also created new spaces of teaching and learning. The shift from the traditional sage on stage to other spaces was not new. Approaches such as distance learning as adopted by the University of South Africa (UNISA) had already seen students being able to study without attending physical classes. However, the rapid development of online technologies allowed new forms of functionality and engagement hitherto not able to be achieved. Universities began to embrace their use and experiment with online course capability in a fast-developing online education market (Love and Fry 2006).

In South Africa, the advance of elearning has been slower. This is in large part due to the barriers to its full use which will be addressed later. However, South Africa has seen a gradual adoption of elearning in a staged manner. The University of KwaZulu-Natal in its *Strategic Plan 2007–2016* determined to 'optimise the use of Information Technology in improving teaching and learning by integrating IT networks and communication protocols into learning environments'. According to Okem (2010) the University of KwaZulu-Natal was committed to the early, appropriate and increased use of information and communication technologies (ICTs) to support teaching and learning. Since then, there has been a steady increase in the adoption of ICTs to support teaching and learning at the university. The use of Moodle (and its rather clunky predecessor, OLS) as an online learning platform has been commonplace for some time and is used in a supplementary fashion to support more traditional on-site lecture-based engagement resulting in a form of blended learning. Blended learning is a hybrid of traditional face-to-face and online learning where instruction happens both in the classroom and online, and where the online component becomes a natural extension of traditional classroom learning (Colis and Moonen 2001).

The Covid-19 lockdown forced the university's hand and demanded an immediate shift from a hybrid to a full elearning model, at least for the duration of the pandemic. Staff and students found themselves facing a daunting task – to build quickly on their skills and knowledge to be able to continue with the curriculum. This meant that the spaces of learning were changing. In the absence of classrooms and physical consultations, lecturers and students had to quickly innovate and adapt to produce the same learning outcomes using an expanded set of electronic modes. This saw the introduction of the use of conference meeting software such as Zoom and Microsoft Teams replacing lectures, and applications such as WhatsApp and email being used for consultations and engagement for students and staff. The latter is an interesting aspect of the change; not only was there a shift in learning spaces but also in spaces of engagement. Gone were the office hours consultation for students or the watercooler-style exchange of ideas for staff. The physical spaces of interaction, idea exchanges and experience-sharing had to find new virtual homes. One such home seemed to readily exist – the WhatsApp group – and this was quickly recognised and co-opted as an accessible, economical and ultimately indispensable way to buttress the scaffolding of the building of new social exchanges and networks. New technologies affect society and its structures and scholars such as Lee and Whitley (2002) argue that the development of technologies (especially ICTs) can affect society dramatically and even serve to change the way we view space and time as factors in our social lives.

Marshall McLuhan famously observed that 'the medium is the message', arguing that the medium of communication is paramount to shaping and understanding the message or content of the communication and, ultimately, the social exchange itself. So, how would a reliance on this new medium change the way in which we share ideas and information? What are the limitations and benefits of using these groups and how can we make sense of these?

WhatsApp for Teaching, Learning and Engagement – Lessons from the Literature

WhatsApp is a free social media platform based on mobile instant messaging (MIM) that allows the creation of groups of participants and sharing of text messages, multimedia files and other documents. It also can be used to make voice calls, video calls and share voice notes.

The use of WhatsApp for direct and supplementary teaching and learning purposes is not new. There have been a number of studies which examine how WhatsApp can be utilised in an educational environment. This section will highlight some of the scholarship and praxis in the area by presenting selected literature.

Baishya and Maheshwari (2020) explored the utilities and burdens associated with educational WhatsApp groups in India. The study highlighted that students were able to successfully use WhatsApp groups to enhance their learning through the exchange of information. It also found that the presence of teachers on the groups constrained the conversation and limited the exchange of ideas. Although the use of WhatsApp groups was seen as burdensome by some learners due to the amount of time needed to read and participate, they were generally seen as positive.

Kee (2020) examined the learning experiences of middle-aged learners, also known as digital immigrants, in an elearning environment in Malaysia. The study found that, for mature students, the formation of WhatsApp groups assisted in supporting learning, although the groups were best suited for peer-to-peer interaction and that the participants still preferred physical interaction with instructors.

Arifani et al. (2020) conducted a comparative study of the use of WhatsApp in English language teaching (ELT) in Indonesia. The authors compared the use of WhatsApp through individual versus collaborative instruction and found that the collaborative group performed significantly higher. This points to the collaborative nature of WhatsApp groups which can produce effective learning outcomes. Similar results were found regarding the positivity of the collaborative aspect of WhatsApp groups in the field of English language teaching by Castrillo, Barcena and Martin-Monje (2014) and Hazea and Alzubi (2016), who saw the use of WhatsApp groups leading to an improvement in students' reading comprehension and essay writing.

Rambe and Bere (2013) examined the use of WhatsApp in an information technology course at a South African university. WhatsApp was used to heighten lecturer-student and peer-based participation, and enhance pedagogical delivery and inclusive learning. The findings showed heightened student participation, the fostering of learning communities for knowledge creation and progressive shifts in the lecturer's mode of pedagogical delivery. The identified challenges included resentment of the merging of academic and family life through WhatsApp consultations after hours and a reticence towards the expansion of WhatsApp's use in other programmes.

Moodley (2019) explored how teachers and officials from a rural district in South Africa used the WhatsApp platform as a virtual community of practice to aid in monitoring and support after attending a professional development programme using a conceptual framework of social learning and social networking. The study highlighted that the effective use of WhatsApp is contingent both on the participants' awareness of the community context and the willingness of the participants to accept differing views and opinions.

Jackson (2020) showed the ability of WhatsApp to bridge the gap in technology provision and enhance students' learning experiences in Sierra Leone with an emphasis on participation in group collaboration, which involves peer-to-peer and peer-to-instructor interaction. The study showed the need for consideration of the digital divide and the limitations of students in terms of literacy and access with particular reference to the availability and cost of internet services.

Further to this point, a study by Koomson (2019) showed that mobile learning using WhatsApp can mitigate the limitations of elearning for Ghanaian students by supplementing more common elearning platforms. The study emphasised the low cost of WhatsApp as an alternative to these platforms and the importance of this for increasing access to elearning for African students. Beyond the direct use of WhatsApp for teaching and learning, WhatsApp can also be used to create small social networks and sites of community engagement.

Doğan (2019) explores this in the examination of school WhatsApp groups comprising teachers and parents in Turkey. Key findings included positive aspects such as lower costs and greater convenience in parent-teacher interaction and negative aspects such as group misuse, conflicts due to misunderstandings, after hours engagement and the minimisation of face-to-face communication.

In a similar study, Zan (2019) looked at the use of WhatsApp communication between teachers and students in Turkish high schools. WhatsApp was found to be positively associated with five key areas: increasing the students' participation, strengthening communication, encouraging information sharing, creating opportunities to learn, and planning the study process. However, the study also revealed drawbacks including disparity in use due to disparate technological and internet access and inappropriate communication styles and language leading to a move to discontinue the use of WhatsApp.

WhatsApp also has the potential to provide a means of activating learning skillsets. This is demonstrated, for example, in the work of Baguma et al. (2019) who showed that WhatsApp was able to help to develop higher order thinking skills like inquiry, creativity, critical reflection and dialogue amongst university students in Ghana using an Activity Theory framework.

Collaborative learning can be enhanced using WhatsApp. This can be shown in the work of Oyewole, Animasahun and Chapman (2020) in their study of the effectiveness of WhatsApp for teaching doctors preparing for a licensing exam in the United Kingdom. Their findings showed a statistically significant improvement in performance on the exam of doctors who were part of a dedicated WhatsApp group and concluded that such groups can be an effective tool for health professional education and can be particularly useful in increasing the motivation to learn.

WhatsApp groups have also been explored in the context of extending learning in a blended environment. Annamalai's (2019) study of a group of undergraduates at a Malaysian university revealed that using WhatsApp groups in this context improved learning outcomes. Negative findings included issues of information fatigue, pedagogical superficiality and technical challenges.

The above studies provide some evidence of the ways in which WhatsApp has been used in an educational context. It is clear that WhatsApp has the potential to both support learning and provide useful spaces of exchange of information and ideas and the collective construction of knowledge. It is also clear that its use can come with some drawbacks – inequitable access in environments of costly or erratic internet, intrusion into the work/life balance, time consumption and irrelevant or inappropriate use among others.

WhatsApp Groups and Social Practice – A Theoretical Perspective

Before examining the use of WhatsApp groups in the context of the School of Social Sciences, it is necessary to develop a theoretical and analytical lens through which their use can be understood. There are a number of theoretical perspectives which could be applied, each asking different types of questions. For this chapter we can look to the broad area of social practice theory. This perspective has been used extensively to analyse social engagement and practice.

Social Practice

Social meaning is inextricable from social practice. The 'things' that we do are imbued with meaning at the individual and social levels. An examination of social practice can highlight these meaning systems. Social practices are routinised behaviours and can be defined as a 'temporally, open-ended set of doings and sayings linked by practical understandings, rules, teleo affective structures and general understandings' (Schatzki 1996: 87). With its roots in the Structuration Theory, Social Practice Theory has as its key proposition that practices are shaped by interconnected elements. For Reckwitz, these elements include: 'forms of bodily activities, forms of mental activities, 'things' and their use, a background knowledge in the form of understanding, know-how, states of emotion and motivational knowledge' (2002: 249). When we frame the use of WhatsApp groups as social practice, we can better understand the doings and meanings around its use.

As a relatively new form of social practice, the use of WhatsApp groups provides insight into the ways in which we adopt and adapt to new ways of doing and thinking. This is particularly important in the context of the global pandemic and can serve as a microcosm of the broader adaptation which was mandated by the rapid structural and pedagogical changes to education delivery during the Covid-19 pandemic. To make sense of these new social practices, a model of analysis needs to be adopted. Following the lead of scholars such as Tyrer (2019), this study draws from Shove et al.'s (2012) three-element model of social practice. This model resonates with the focus of the study as the analysis presented herein is that of reported reflections on the use of WhatsApp groups and not a content analysis of the groups themselves. By adopting this model, we can examine and understand the interplay between the three elements in the use of WhatsApp groups for pedagogical support. In Social Practice Theory, individuals are not the units of analysis but rather are seen as the carriers of a practice (Reckwitz 2002a). This model provides a categorical basis for the explication of social practice by outlining three key elements of analysis: materials, meaning and competencies.

Materials

This element highlights the role and importance of materials or artefacts in social practices. Reckwitz (2002b) argues that practices involve interaction with non-human 'things'. The nature of the material aspects of the social practice affects the practice itself.

Meaning

When we engage in social practices, we operate with a shared set of understandings about how these should be carried out. This meaning-making is rooted in Bourdieu's construct of habitus which he defined as 'a set of dispositions, reflexes and forms of behaviour that people acquire through acting in society' (2000: 19). Individuals create these understandings through their life experiences and respond to new practices accordingly while adapting meaning according to context.

Competencies

Competencies are at the intersection of materials and meaning – knowing how to physically engage with the materials of a social practice is important and social actors build on this by translating meaning into praxis. Knowing the conventions of a social practice shapes the nature of the practice. Actors need to develop these competencies through meaning making and shared feedback over time. These competencies shape and are shaped by the shared 'rules' which develop when practice becomes routinised.

These elements will be revisited later in the discussion and will serve to give insight into the key findings.

WhatsApp in the School of Social Sciences during Covid-19

This section will focus on the use of WhatsApp groups in the School of Social Sciences during the Covid-19 pandemic. It will begin by examining the types of groups formed. It will then discuss student experiences of these groups through a reflection on a student survey. This will be followed by reflections of academic staff on the use of these groups.

Typologies of WhatsApp groups in the School of Social Sciences

WhatsApp groups are diverse in their nature. The type of group, the membership, the level of formality and the intended purpose create varied typologies. This section will briefly outline the dominant group typologies. The focus will be on those groups that at least partly contribute to the advancement of teaching and learning and will exclude other common types such as purely social or externally located groups.

Student Class Groups

These groups are formed by the students of a particular course. Their membership is limited to students only. Their purpose is varied but largely involves sharing information about and discussing course-related topics such as course material, assignments, updates and so forth. These are informal groups although they are often managed by, or at least include, class representatives who are then able to bring issues and problems raised in the group to the lecturer and then transmit the response back into the group. The inclusion of students only allows a more open participation away from the gaze of the lecturer.

Student-Academic Class Groups

These groups consist of students and the lecturer/s of a course. They are usually formed by the lecturer or class representative. Their purpose is to discuss issues arising from the course and students are able to address questions and problems directly in the group with the lecturer/s. They are more formal in nature and do not encourage off-topic discussion. The inclusion of the lecturer usually discourages unnecessary, irrelevant or inappropriate content. A sub-set of this typology would be tutorial groups where the tutor of the course may have a separate group for discussion of the tutorial topics.

Formal Staff Groups

These groups consist of university staff, usually a mixture of academic and administrative staff, although there may be academic-only or administrative-only sub-types. They are usually formed by the leader of the group or a designate and their purpose is to share information, experiences and updates with each other. The groups are formal and dedicated to primarily work-related posts although the natural inclination to engage with more personal issues is often expressed, for example celebrating a birthday or sending condolences on a loss. These groups often have high levels of participation. These groups are structured hierarchically. For example, in the School of Social Sciences there is a WhatsApp group which includes all staff in the school. There can also be smaller groups formed on the basis of organisational structure, for example groups created at the 'cluster' level in which staff of a particular set of cognate disciplines are able to discuss issues relating to their particular cluster. Below the cluster level there may also be disciplinary groups consisting of academics from a particular discipline or programme. Other examples of formal staff groups can be seen in groups that are created to facilitate a particular activity, project or mandate. Examples of these may be groups created by committees, research groups or task teams. During the Covid-19 pandemic these groups are key sites of the exchange of ideas and information. This exchange will sometimes be supplemented by other communicative modes such as email.

Informal Staff Groups

These groups are created by academics for non-teaching-related purposes. Although they are not directly related to teaching and learning, their usefulness warrants a mention. These groups are voluntary and created as 'social groups' in which staff can share non-work-related information. The benefits of these groups are to maintain the social cohesion which existed before the lockdown. These are informal groups and are created on an ad hoc-basis. Content is varied but common topics are the social and political landscape, discussion of families and events and information about the pandemic. Humour is a common theme with staff sometimes posting jokes, memes or anecdotes. The importance of maintaining social capital and reinforcing shared values during a pandemic should not be understated. These groups support a positive institutional culture and strengthen ties between staff as well as provide moral or emotional support. Questions which might seem out of place or inappropriate in a more formal group could be posed here.

Broadcast Groups and Hybridity

A WhatsApp broadcast group is formed when a user creates a list of recipients and saves it as a broadcast list. The user can then send a message or file to the group and it is sent to all members. The key difference to a regular WhatsApp group is that the recipients cannot see who else is receiving the message and if they reply to the message, it is seen only by the original user. This type of group is best suited for a hierarchical, primarily one-way type of communication. Lecturers may elect to rely on this type of group to send updates, files and information to a class of recipients where there is no need for discussion or engagement.

An approach that has been used by some lecturers is to have hybridity in their use of WhatsApp. An effective model has proved to be the creation of a student class group sans the lecturer to allow engagement without interference from the lecturer and then, alongside this group, the creation of a formal broadcast group to send information and resources to students. Thus, management of the class group is led by the students and management of the broadcast content is managed by the lecturer.

Student Experiences of WhatsApp Groups – Reflections on a Student Survey

As discussed earlier, the School of Social Sciences at the University of KwaZulu-Natal set up an online learning task team to respond to the Covid-19 pandemic by providing information and support to staff as they moved to new forms of online learning. The task team developed and administered a survey in April 2020 which sought to explore the students' readiness for online learning. The data was used to inform and guide the school's response to the shifting modalities of teaching and learning in higher education. All students in the school were sent a link to the online survey and a total of 456 usable responses were analysed. Given the school's student enrolment of 4,771 students, this sample size was sufficient to ensure a 95% confidence level with a 5% margin of error. Selected results of the survey will be presented here to form a basis for discussion of the use of WhatsApp as a support mechanism for teaching and learning.

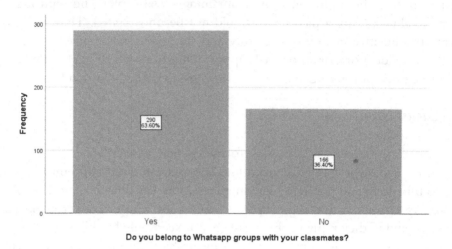

Figure 1: Belongs to course WhatsApp groups (n=456)

Figure 1 shows that at the beginning of the lockdown about two-thirds (63.6%) of students already belonged to course WhatsApp groups. These groups would typically be formed organically by students and would seldom include lecturers. They would primarily be used for students to share information about their courses with each other and included sharing dates of tests, questions about the course or curriculum and so forth. These existing groups suddenly moved from supplementary spaces which supported more conventional forms of information sharing to the primary sites of engagement for students. In the situation of uncertainty and change facing students who had moved off-campus and away from their physical social networks, these groups became important sources of information and even comfort as they were able to share common problems and experiences. Students were asked to reflect on the benefits of these student groups and the qualitative responses were coded and are presented in Figure 2 above. The main identified benefits of the groups were information sharing (34.6%) followed by updates (24.6%), discussion, problem solving and debate and assistance with assignments/revision (12.8%). Information about the course and updates on the evolving and shifting rules and expectations necessitated by the Covid-19 pandemic was crucial in assisting students to stay abreast of developments. This was particularly necessary in the early months of the

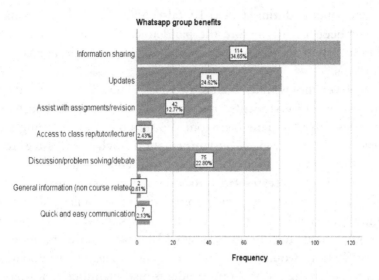

Figure 2: Benefits of course WhatsApp groups (multiple response variable; coded from qualitative responses)

lockdown where the university would often change the goalposts by shifting assignment requirements and dates for submissions, etc. The identification of discussion, problem solving and debate as a benefit shows that these groups had the ability to not only serve as spaces of information exchange but also, as indicated by the literature, sites of idea exchange and debate and the development of higher order thinking and engagement. Ideas can be presented and discussed in real time and through this exchange, students are able to collectively create shared understandings. These groups are often populated by the majority of the class and so students are able to get many more perspectives on issues, such as assignment preparation, than would normally be the case with the more limited-in-size physical social networks of friends and acquaintances in the classroom setting. One student's response identified the importance of her 'Corona buddies', a term which describes

| | | Responses | | Percent of Cases |
		N	Percent	
Whatsapp challenges	Data/connectivity issues	85	36.6%	42.7%
	Irrelevant posts	90	38.8%	45.2%
	Misinformation	11	4.7%	5.5%
	Lack of participation/reponses	25	10.8%	12.6%
	Confusion/misunderstanding	21	9.1%	10.6%
Total		232	100.0%	116.6%

Table 3: Challenges of course WhatsApp groups (multiple response variable; coded from 232 qualitative responses)

friends made online during Covid-19 (also known as the Coronavirus) who had not been friends before the pandemic. The development of real friendships and support networks in an online space is an interesting aspect of these groups.

The groups were not without their drawbacks. Figure 3 shows the identified disadvantages raised by students. The main concern was the existence of irrelevant posts (38.8%). This bears out the findings from existing studies. The inclusion of irrelevant posts and information (such as excessive chatting) can clutter the groups and make it more difficult to analyse the useful information. This also creates frustration at the constant intrusion of the group into the lives of students when notifications are regularly alerting them to new messages which often turn out to be unnecessary postings. Some students complained that the groups would be active after hours and the flood of notifications would be an irritation. This can lead to group fatigue or even resentment of the group. Some students also identified that there were certain members of the group that would hijack discussions and have back-and-forth exchanges within the group which all members would be privy to. This indicates a need for the development of established guidelines and the creation of a protocol of online etiquette. The burden of this would be placed on the administrator/s who started the group. As the use of these groups are in a nascent stage, there is only an inchoate understanding of what should be allowed and what should be excluded as well as, possibly, the repercussion of violations of these rules. One class representative reported having to remove members for unspecified inappropriate behaviour. The idea of virtual spaces problematises the acceptance of standard norms and mores within a group. As the group is seen as an important space, it will be inhabited by students with diverse backgrounds and social and cultural practices. As WhatsApp groups were largely social before the pandemic, the move to bring them closer into the pedagogical fold requires institutions to carefully consider the ethical challenges they may pose. Behaviour such as harassment has been reported and there are no clear guidelines in place for the management of such occurrences. A recommendation might be to formalise these groups into the curriculum. For example, the class representative could be tasked with forming and managing the 'official' class group which would have clear guidelines of use and established sanctions for non-compliance. The class would then be free to create concurrent informal groups which would be free of these guidelines. The identification of confusion and misunderstanding (9.1%) and misinformation (4.7%) speaks to a broader problem with social media. Other social media spaces such as Facebook are often criticised for the spread of misinformation or even 'fake news', where members, knowingly or unknowingly, post incorrect or misleading information. WhatsApp groups are not immune to this. Some students (10.8%) saw a lack of participation or response in groups as problematic. Students cited the lack of responses to questions as a problem or that groups were stagnant with little participation. The lack of data or connectivity was raised by about a third (36.6%) of respondents. This is a serious stumbling block to equitable and meaningful online learning and is often encapsulated with reference to the 'digital divide' which exists in South Africa. The movement of students out of residences and back to their homes created a situation where some students could not reliably access online learning due to poor network signal, a lack of data, a lack of appropriate devices or combinations of these three problems. This challenge will form the basis of a later section of the chapter.

Academics' Experiences of WhatsApp groups

Online teaching and learning necessitated by the Covid-19 pandemic involves both students and lecturers becoming accustomed to new ways of pedagogical thinking and doing. Although WhatsApp was not an uncommon platform to academic staff, for many lecturers the use of WhatsApp and WhatsApp groups for teaching and learning purposes was a novel idea and practice. Those lecturers who had used the platform beforehand had used it as a supplementary tool and not as the primary mode of communication. In an online discussion at the end of the first semester, academic staff were able to discuss their experiences and the lessons learned during this tumultuous time. This discussion broached a broad array of topics. This section will briefly discuss the key points which relate to WhatsApp and WhatsApp groups.

There is a general consensus that the use of WhatsApp was a necessary and useful element in the adoption of online teaching and learning. Most lecturers were using both staff and staff-student groups. Staff were happy with the ease, reliability and immediacy of information sharing that WhatsApp provides. The use of voice notes (recording a sending an audio file) was viewed positively whereas typing a long response is time consuming. Being able to see when a recipient has received and read sent messages was also useful.

Beyond convenience, some staff pointed to a sense of closeness and empathy being in contact with students can provide. It allows an insight into the lived experiences of students which was heightened by the social and economic turmoil being experienced.

Some staff have used WhatsApp not just as a supplementary platform of teaching but more directly as the medium of instruction, posting threads of videos and text around a lesson for students to engage with. These types of experiments can serve to develop the pedagogical insights and techniques of academics.

WhatsApp was also a primary mode of communication used when supervising postgraduate students. The use of voice calling and video calling provided a cheap and effective means to maintain supervisory relationships with students. In response to this, the Online Learning Task Team developed and distributed a guide to WhatsApp video calling for staff. WhatsApp was also used in at least one postgraduate course for students to record and send presentations to the lecturer in the form of an audio file.

In terms of the drawbacks, the main issue was that of work–life balance. The blurring of work and home life is exacerbated in an environment of constant and immediate access to academics and some expressed fatigue from belonging to too many groups and being unable to effectively manage their personal time. The use of data necessitated by the new online forms of teaching and learning was also a general point which relates somewhat to WhatsApp although this was raised primarily in respect to more data-intensive platforms such as Zoom.

The Digital Divide

Having shown the potentials of and experiences with WhatsApp groups as a supplementary pedagogical tool, it is important to address the elephant in the room – the digital divide. It is hard to find a discussion of online learning which does not raise this.

The digital divide can be simply considered to refer to the 'gap between those people who have access to digital technologies and information via the internet, and those who do not' (Singh 2004: 5). This gap is characterised by two intertwined elements – *access* and *literacy*. Access deals with the inequitable diffusion of and access to digital resources such as devices (laptops, smartphones, etc.) and data or internet access. Literacy refers to the ability of users to easily and meaningfully employ these devices for their intended purposes. The argument is simple: in an environment where there is inequitable access to, and literacy of, technology, elearning has the potential to further entrench the existing divide in society and create a situation where those with limited access and/or literacy are further marginalised and even excluded from teaching and learning.

This is not a spurious concern. Even though the move to online learning during the Covid-19 pandemic was not planned and was necessitated by events beyond the university's control, it is important to recognise and try to mitigate the challenges that the digital divide among students can bring.

But what does this divide look like in South Africa among the student body? Before the pandemic, the university had put measures in place to narrow the gap such as providing free Wi-Fi on campus and rolling out the provision of laptops to students. Under the pandemic though, students were alienated from the campus and its resources and were dispersed to their homes throughout the province and country. Some selected findings from the student survey can give us some clarity as to the effects of this and will be grouped into issues of access and literacy respectively.

Access

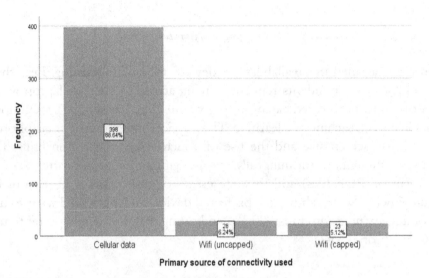

Figure 4: Primary source of connectivity to Internet (n=456)

Figure 4 determined the primary source of connectivity to the internet among students. The vast majority reported that their primary source of connectivity was cellular data (88.6%). The implications of this for online learning is that as cellular data is more costly and more erratic than Wi-Fi, and there is a need to reduce the cost of online access. Although the university did provide students with a monthly cellular data package, this was often quickly used up as they engaged using data intensive software like Zoom to hold classes.

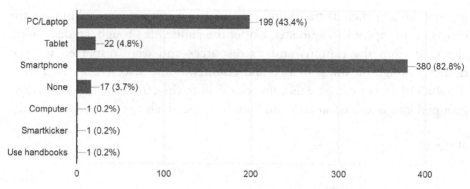

Figure 5: Figure 3.5 Available devices for online learning (multiple response variable)

Figure 5 examined the availability of devices for online learning. Less than half (43%) of respondents reported having access to a PC or laptop while 83% of students reported having a smartphone. This has serious implications for delivery of teaching and learning. The physical limitations of smartphones in terms of screen size and the use of touch screen navigation limits the ability of students to meaningfully engage with course notes (often sent in the form of PDF files) and to write essays or tests. This is borne out by Figure 6 below which shows the preferred device students would want to use for online learning with most (90.3%) indicating that they would prefer to use a PC or laptop device.

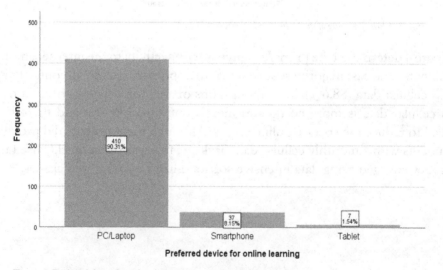

Figure 6: Preferred device for online learning (n=454)

This disconnect between what they have and what would be ideal further entrenched the idea that the way in which we provide teaching and learning in the school during Covid-19 needed to move from the traditional to the pragmatic. As a school we needed to ensure that we took into consideration the limitations of access and device and move to create learning and communication spaces which are more suited for use on mobile or cellular devices.

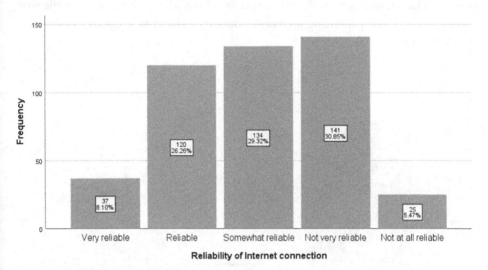

Figure 7: Reliability of Internet Connection (n=457)

Figure 7 shows the reported reliability of the available internet connection by students. Just over a third (36.32%) of students reported having an internet connection that was not very reliable or not at all reliable. Clearly access to devices and the internet posed issues for students.

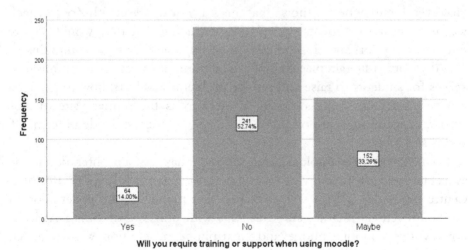

Figure 8: Requires training or support for Moodle (n=457)

Literacy

The hybrid approach to teaching and learning adopted by the university pre-shutdown resulted in students being somewhat prepared to use online modes. The dominant platforms used by the university were Moodle for course management (posting lectures, notes, assessments, etc.) and Zoom for conducting online classes.

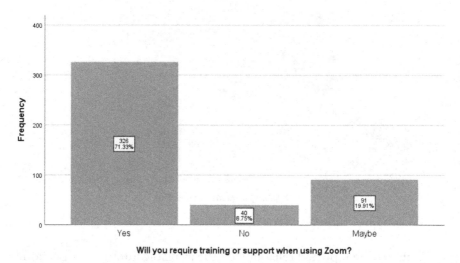

Figure 9: Requires training or support for Zoom (n=457)

Figure 8 indicates that students were largely prepared for the use of Moodle with only 14% reporting that they would require training or support. However, Figure 9 below shows that this was not the case with Zoom which was unfamiliar to students with 71.3% indicating that they would require training or support and close to 20% indicating that they may require this.

This disparity of literacy places emphasis on the importance of communicative spaces for students to raise and resolve problems and learn how to properly use new software such as Zoom. WhatsApp as the primary site of this engagement becomes important in addressing the digital divide in terms of access and literacy.

The progress of technological advancement has seen a proliferation in the availability and affordability of mobile devices. According to a Pew Research Centre report, in 2018 it was estimated that mobile phone penetration in the South African market stood at 91% with only 9% of South Africans not owning a mobile phone and smartphone penetration was estimated at 51%. A smartphone is a mobile device that performs similar functions to a computer and has internet access and an operating system capable of running downloaded applications such as email and social media applications including WhatsApp.

WhatsApp has a high degree of penetration in the South African market with 58 per cent of South African mobile phone owners using the app as of February 2020 (Statista, n.d.). A comparison of data usage across video messaging platforms by Business Insider has found that WhatsApp is the most economical mode of delivery (Caboz, 2020). The ubiquity of WhatsApp can be attributed, in part, to its low cost compared to other forms of communication. Users can make calls and send messages that incur relatively small data costs. According to the Independent Communications Authority of South Africa (ICASA) in its analysis of flat rate per second billing tariff plans in South Africa, the cost of a phone call for one minute ranges from R0,66 to R2.00. The cost of an average voice call using WhatsApp ranges from R0.02 to R0.06 per minute. (ICASA 2018).

Thus, WhatsApp can be seen as a bridge through which the digital divide can be mitigated. Its ubiquity and cheapness make it an ideal platform on which students can collectively learn how to best participate in teaching and learning.

Discussion and Conclusion

The above analysis is of descriptive interest but can also be understood through the lens of social practice. In the data we see the intersection of meaning, competencies and materials as would be expected when adopting a new social practice. It is clear that the transition from traditional to online learning reinvigorated the meaning making around our online actions and devices. WhatsApp groups went from voluntary and supplementary spaces to quasi-official pedagogical spaces. Participants in these spaces had to re-evaluate their user-pattens and norms accordingly. The disparity of material factors (such as the availability of data, access to smartphones, laptops, etc.) led to differential modes of access and engagement and in this regard the digital divide can be seen as a function of a divide of materials (access) and competencies (literacy).

The sudden reliance on WhatsApp as a learning tool led to a reframing of its usefulness and modes of meaning making around what constitutes learning and the separation of learning from fixed spatial places. Along with the benefits came drawbacks (as discussed above). These drawbacks are largely rooted in the collective project of social practice. As technology and online engagement develop, we see the emergence of new social norms, mores and practices around its use. In the context of the Covid-19 pandemic, students and staff alike were not afforded the luxury of an incremental and shared development of rules of practice and transitional optionality. Participants in this nascent social practice were seen to be naturally frustrated at the new ways of being and doing. The intrusion into personal lives, the existence of irrelevant or unnecessary content and the limitations of the 'small screen classroom' can be seen as an operational artefact of collective uncertainty over the 'rules of the game' that normally would develop more organically. Degrees of familiarity with conventions and expectations varied as students and staff alike sought to claim these online spaces. These challenges related to materials, meanings and competencies highlight the particularity and peculiarity of new forms of pedagogical spaces. Compounding this is the adoption of WhatsApp groups for teaching and learning that vary in their typologies (see typology discussion above). Although the use of such groups has been framed primarily as novel spaces, it should be noted that social actors engaging in these spaces are not without a frame of reference – the existence of other online spaces (email, internet forums, etc.) mean that there are existing patterns of meaning and understanding that can be co-opted and serve as a basis for expansion. Over time as we learn to incorporate these practices into mainstream teaching and learning, it is hoped that the drawbacks will be mitigated and the benefits enhanced. While material access is likely to exist as an ongoing issue, the making of meaning and the development of competencies should be expected to improve.

This chapter has provided some insight into the adoption of online teaching and learning during the Covid-19 pandemic. It has emphasised the use and usefulness of WhatsApp and WhatsApp groups as supplementary spaces of exchange and engagement. It is expected that this use will deepen even after the return to normality. If this is the case, the lessons learned need to be carefully thought through. It is clear that WhatsApp has the potential to support teaching and learning. It is also clear that this use can and does come at a cost. If we are to bring WhatsApp into the institutional fold, we need to ensure that we strike a balance between the advantages and disadvantages of its use. A recommendation is that we try to reduce the latter through the development and adoption of guidelines which govern its use. It is also recommended that further scholarship be encouraged in this area to provide a basis for best practice.

References

Annamalai, N. (2019) 'Using WhatsApp to extend learning in a blended classroom environment', *Teaching English with Technology*, Vol. 19, No. 1, pp. 3–20.

Arifani, Y., Asari, S., Anwar, K and Budianto, L. (2020) 'Individual or collaborative "WhatsApp" learning? A flipped classroom model of EFL writing instruction', *Teaching English with Technology*. No. 20, pp. 122–139.

Baishya, D. and Maheshwari, S. (2020) 'WhatsApp groups in academic context: Exploring the academic uses of WhatsApp groups among students', *Contemporary Educational Technology*. Vol. 11, No. 1, pp. 31–46.

Baguma, R., Bagarukayo, E., Namubiru, P., Brown, C. and Mayisela, T. (2019) 'Using WhatsApp in teaching to develop higher order thinking skills – a literature review using the Activity Theory lens', *International Journal of Education and Development using Information and Communication Technology (IJEDICT)*, Vol. 15, No. 2, pp. 98–116.

Bourdieu, P. (2000) 'The politics of protest. An interview with Kevin Ovenden', *Socialist Review*. http://pubs.socialistreviewindex.org.uk/sr242/ovenden.htm (accessed 30 August 2020).

Caboz, J. (2020) 'Compared: SA video calls on Zoom, Skype, Teams, Hangouts and WhatsApp, https://www.businessinsider.co.za/heres-why-your-video-conference-app-keeps-acting-up-recommended-bandwidth-speeds-of-zoom-microsoft-teams-skype-google-hangouts-met-and-whatsapp-2020-4 (accessed 30 August 2020).

Castrillo, M., Barcena, E. and Martin M. E. (2014) 'New forms of negotiating meaning on the move: The use of mobile-based chatting for foreign language distance learning', *LADIS International Journal of WWW/Internet*, Vol. 12, No. 2, pp. 51–67.

Colis, B. and Moonen, J. (2001) *Flexible learning in a digital world: Experiences and expectations*, London: Kogan-Page.

Czerniewicz, L. and Brown, C. (2010) 'Strengthening and Weakening Boundaries: Students Negotiating Technology Mediated learning', in R. Sharpe, H. Beetham. and S. de Freitas (eds) *Rethinking Learning for a Digital Age – How Learners are Shaping their Own Experiences*, New York: Routledge.

Davis, S. and Botkin, D. (1994) *Monsters under the Bed*, New York: Touchstone.

Doğan, S. (2019) 'The changing face of organisational communication: School WhatsApp groups, *Research in Pedagogy*, Vol. 9, No. 2, pp. 231–244.

Hazea, A. and Alzubi, A. (2016) 'The effectiveness of using mobile on EFL learners' reading practices in Najran University', *English Language Teaching*, Vol. 9, No. 5, pp. 8–21.

Independent Communications Authority of South Africa (ICASA) (2018) Bi-Annual Report on the Analysis of Tariff Notifications Submitted to ICASA for the Period of 01 July 2018 to 31 December 2018, *https://www.icasa.org.za/uploads/files/Q4-Bi-annual-Tariff-Analysis-Report-jul-dec2018.pdf* (accessed 22 August 2020).

Jackson, E. (2020) 'Use of WhatsApp for flexible learning: Its effectiveness in supporting teaching and learning in Sierra Leone's Higher Education Institutions', *International Journal of Advanced Corporate Learning*, Vol. 13, No. 1, pp. 35–47.

Kee, Ch'ng, L. (2020) 'Face-to-face tutorials, learning management system and WhatsApp group: How digital immigrants interact and engage in e-learning?', *Malaysian Online Journal of Educational Technology*, No. 8, pp. 18–35.

Koomson, W. (2019) 'Ontology of Ubiquitous Learning: WhatsApp Messenger Competes Successfully with Learning Management Systems (LMS) in Ghana', 10.33965/icedutech2019_201902L009, pp. 75–82.

Lee, H. and Whitley, E. (2002) 'Time and information technology: Temporal impacts on individuals, organizations, and society', *The Information Society*, No. 18, pp. 235–240.

Love, N. and Fry, N. (2006) 'Accounting students' perceptions of a virtual learning environment: Springboard or safety net?', *Accounting Education*, Vol. 15, No. 2, pp. 151–166.

Moodley, M. (2019) 'WhatsApp: Creating a virtual teacher community for supporting and monitoring after a professional development programme', *South African Journal of Education*. Vol. 39, No. 2, pp. 1–10.

OECD (2005) *E-learning in tertiary education*, http://www.oecd.org/education/ceri/35991871.pdf (accessed 1 September 2020).

Okem, A. (2010) A Policy Analysis of E-learning at the University of KwaZulu-Natal, unpublished Masters Dissertation, Policy and Development Studies, University of KwaZulu-Natal.

Oyewole, B, Animasahun, V. and Chapman, H. (2020) 'A survey on the effectiveness of WhatsApp for teaching doctors preparing for a licensing exam', *PLoS ONE*, Vol. 15, No. 4, pp. 1–9.

Pew Research Centre (2018) 'Internet Connectivity Seen as Having Positive Impact on Life in Sub-Saharan Africa', https://www.pewresearch.org/global/2018/10/09/majorities-in-sub-saharan-africa-own-mobile-phones-but-smartphone-adoption-is-modest/ (accessed 22 August 2020).

Rambe, P. and Bere, A. (2013) 'Using mobile instant messaging to leverage learner participation and transform pedagogy at a South African University of Technology', *British Journal of Educational Technology*, Vol. 44, No. 4, pp. 544–561.

Reckwitz, A. (2002a) 'Toward a theory of social practices: A development in culturalist theorizing', *European Journal of Social Theory*, Vol. 5, No. 2, pp. 243–263.

Reckwitz, A. (2002b) 'The status of the "material" in theories of culture. From "social structure" to "artefact"', *Journal for the Theory of Social Behaviour*, No. 32, pp. 195–217.

Rovai, A. and Jordan, H. (2004) 'Blended learning and sense of community: A comparative analysis with traditional and fully online graduate courses', *The International Review of Research in Open and Distributed Learning*, Vol. 5, No. 2, pp. 1–13.

Shove, E., Pantzar, M. and Watson, M. (2012) *The Dynamics of Social Practice: Everyday life and how it changes*, London: Sage.

Singh, A. (2004) 'Bridging the digital divide: the role of universities in getting South Africa closer to the global information society', *South African Journal of Information Management*, Vol. 6, No. 2, pp. 1-9.

Statista (n.d.) Most popular mobile apps used in South Africa as of February 2020, by reach, https://www.statista.com/statistics/1103151/most-popular-mobile-apps-south-africa (accessed 30 August 2020).

Tyrer, C. (2019) 'Beyond social chit chat? Analysing the social practice of a mobile messaging service on a higher education teacher development course', *International Journal of Educational Technology in Higher Education*, No. 16, p. 13.

University of KwaZulu-Natal (2007) *Strategic Plan 2007–2016*.

Zan, N. (2019) 'Communication channels between teachers and students in chemistry education: WhatsApp', *US-China Education Review*, Vol. 9, No. 1, pp. 18–30.

Chapter 3

Pursuing an Ethics of Care and a Pedagogy of Compassion during Crisis

Kathryn Pillay and Shaun Ruggunan
University of KwaZulu-Natal

Introduction

This chapter makes a contribution to the current scholarship on ethics of care in academia by arguing that the current Covid-19 pandemic has amplified the need for an ethics of care in the way universities and academics engage with students and peers during crisis. An ethics of care broadly refers to the priority of relationships, concern and responsibility for others as opposed to concern only about utilitarian outcomes (passing or failing a course, for example). The chapter claims that self-care and care for the other are not mutually exclusive practices during crises. We further contend that developing an ethics of care and pedagogy of compassion is a necessary if underexplored part of the decolonisation debate of higher education in South Africa. The decolonisation project in South Africa tends to focus on issues of curriculum content and higher education access and less on an ethics of care as applied to the self and the other. We employ collaborative autoethnography as our method to make our contribution. The chapter begins by providing a background and context to the current global crisis, and the higher education context in South Africa. In so doing, it explores the ways in which we think about decoloniality in higher education, ethics of care and compassionate pedagogy. Following on from this, the chapter will be organised around two questions posed by this study: (1) Why is an ethics of care approach necessary in the South African context? and (2) How might an ethics of care and compassionate pedagogy be practised by academics in higher education?

Background

The global health emergency brought on by the coronavirus (SARS-CoV-2) pandemic, which causes the respiratory disease Covid-19 has reconstituted daily activities in ways many living through it would not have imagined in their lifetime. The rapid spread of Covid-19 across the world has resulted in many countries, including South Africa, implementing lockdown and quarantine measures such as stay at home orders and travel bans to curb the spread of the virus via community transmission within its borders, and to also prevent new cases from entering. United Nations (UN) Secretary General, António Guterres, described the pandemic as '… an economic crisis. A social crisis. And a human crisis that is fast becoming a human rights crisis' with the UN referring to it as the worst humanitarian crisis since World War Two (Guterres 2020: par. 2). In South Africa particularly, lockdown measures, supported by the military and increased police presence, have meant the closing of all non-essential businesses including both the basic education and higher education sectors (John 2020).[1] The ramifications of this global pandemic have rendered it a unique crisis in modern times, and the full extent of the physical, mental and emotional consequences for the world's population remain to be seen.

In South Africa, the pandemic has exposed the deepening fissures of structural and income inequality, including unequal access to education. The response by universities throughout the world, including South Africa, however, has been swift, resulting in quick closure of campuses and residences, and a sharp shift to remote online teaching in the space of a few weeks. South Africa is a profoundly unequal society and these inequities are reflected in its universities. A simple shift towards online teaching or emergency remote teaching and learning to mitigate against pandemic-initiated lockdowns and social distancing policies, therefore, is not by itself a sufficient response. Universities invoke the language of neo-liberal new managerialism[2] when describing their responses as strategies to ensure 'business continuity' to serve their customers (students). This is reflective of embedded new managerial policies that have come to shape South African universities since the mid-1990s (Webster and Mosoetsa 2002; Anderson 2003; Ntshoe et al. 2008; Magoqwana et al. 2019). South African universities have responded to the pandemic through the prism of embedded new managerialist cultures. This is contrary to some claims that the pandemic seeded new managerialist cultures at universities. By the beginning of 2020, this form of management style coupled with the massification of higher education had already been entrenched for almost two decades. The pandemic rendered some of these practices more visible.

Managerialist approaches to teaching and learning, however, threaten the social justice dimensions of the humanities.[3] Therefore in the race to continue with the operations of the university as 'business', the complexity of the socio-economic challenges faced by academic staff and students need to be considered. Higher education institutions cannot ignore the pre-pandemic environments of staff and, more especially, students. Responses to teaching and learning must be considerate of the 'limits of agency structured by race, class, nationality, ability, sexuality, and so on' (Weil 2020: par. 14).

Compounding this is a crisis in higher education institutions around South Africa presently, which is manifested by ongoing student protests.[4] For instance, calls for the decolonisation of the curriculum in South African universities, highlight the protracted struggle for social justice and equality, 25 years after the democratic transition. The global disruption brought on by the Covid-19 pandemic not only foregrounds these debates, but highlights the academic imperative to employ decolonising pedagogies and teaching philosophies underpinned by an ethics of care. The present crisis offers a unique and urgent opportunity for social scientists to develop a more socially just and compassionate response to challenges faced in higher education.

We wish to extend the definition of ethics of care provided earlier on to explicitly include two additional features of an ethics of care. First an ethics of care must necessarily be anti new managerialist practices and second it must be informed by decoloniality, especially for academies situated in the global South. This coincides with employing pedagogies for social justice more specifically as a critical compassionate pedagogy which according to Hao (2011: 92) is 'a pedagogical commitment that allows educators to criticize institutional and classroom practices that ideologically underserve students at disadvantaged positions, while at the same time be self-reflexive of their actions through compassion as a daily commitment'. When taken together, enacting an ethics of care and engaging in a pedagogy of compassion, higher education institutions and academics can provide an inclusive teaching and learning space that favours equitable outcomes for all students.

Concurrent Collaborative Autoethnography as Method

Autoethnography as a form of reflexive inquiry in qualitative research is well established. It involves a dialogic conversation between the self (auto) and societal context (ethno) that the researcher is exploring (Ellis, Adams and Bochner 2011). When we write down our interpretation of this in narrative and analytical form, we then engage the 'graphy' component of the method (Ellis, Adams and Bochner 2011). The self-reflection, however, needs to be less inward gazing and rather transformed through the lens of the sociological imagination. It is this process of self-reflection intersecting with the sociological imagination that allows an accessing of the personal to extend the sociological imagination about social issues in the researcher's discipline (Kinnear and Ruggunan 2019: 2). The appeal for a more analytic autoethnography over the last two decades resulted in a variation of collaborative styles of autoethnography (Chang et al. 2016). These range from duoethnography to community autoethnographies (Chang et al. 2016). These forms of autoethnography prioritise the relationships amongst different selves and society rather than prioritising a 'master narrative of one self' (Chang et al. 2016: 48). In other words, all collaborators become informants or researcher-participants in the study as multiple selves dialogue with the research problem identified by the research team.

For this study we adopted a concurrent model of collaborative autoethnography. Conventional qualitative and quantitative approaches, such as surveys and in-depth interviews, do not allow for a centring of the self in research. The deliberate choice of our methodology unpacks how an ethics of care has shaped our academic careers during this crisis. The collaboration was between the two of us (Kathryn Pillay and Shaun Ruggunan). We both work at the University of KwaZulu-Natal (UKZN) as academics even though we are based in different colleges.[5] We are two academics who have similar trajectories at UKZN, having both done our undergraduate studies at the former University of Natal, and thereafter completed our Masters degrees together in the Industrial, organisational and labour studies discipline. While we both did not begin our careers in academia at the same time, we both have, nevertheless, been employed only at UKZN. We both have long histories at the university as students and staff. Our experience with UKZN pre- and post-merger totals 25 years each, with 19 years being in the employ of the university. This length of time means we have institutional memory and are intimately familiar with the changing university culture over the years. We write from these identities. In addition, Shaun's spouse worked throughout the lockdown as a frontline worker, and Kathryn's spouse returned to work during the level-4 lockdown while her daughter returned to school soon after, adding to the anxiety during this period. Kathryn's identities as mother and a woman also shaped her experiences of work during this time.

Both of us are experiencing the same challenges in teaching, learning and university managerial style during the pandemic albeit in different campuses of our university. The impetus for this chapter was organic with both of us accumulating a substantial quantity of voice notes, telephone conversations, online chats and Zoom meetings discussing the research questions posed by this study. These various platforms of engagement produced a large data corpus between 12 March 2020 and the time of submission of this chapter for publication.

Data Collection and Analyses

The data collection was divided into four categories that took place simultaneously.

1. face-to-face meetings on Zoom;
2. WhatsApp chat discussions;
3. WhatsApp voice notes;
4. shared Google drive as a repository for secondary data relevant to the study.

Most CAE studies will have planned discrete phases of data collection (Hernandez, Wambura Ngunjiri and Chang 2015) but in our case the organic nature of the various discussions across various synchronous and asynchronous platforms (which we subsequently treat as data) was simultaneous. Our combined self-reflection as well as dialogical reflection of each other in relation to the research questions informed our data reduction and analysis strategies.

Nonetheless as a sense-making strategy we retrospectively engaged in the following processes. Whilst the theory/concepts/values informing this study were always implicit, the processes outlined below made these explicit. This allows also for greater levels of transparency and trustworthiness of the reportage. We organised this in the following phases:

1. In Phase 1 we constructed culturegrams (Hernandez, Wambura Ngunjiri and Chang 2015) which are conceptual maps of our identities. We wrote down what we think are the important self-markers of our identity (for example, race, gender, rank, tenure, parental status, marital status). We then individually wrote down a narrative that responds to our research question using a critical incident reporting method. In other words, what were the critical incidents we experienced individually that prompted us to engage the research question of this study. We then shared these pieces of writing with each other.

2. In Phase 2 we reflected on each other's writing and had a Zoom discussion about commonalities and differences of experiences.

3. We then also decided how to manage and organise the data corpus on the various digital platforms we were using.

4. In Phase 3 we exported WhatsApp chats with time stamps into Word to make it more accessible, and the Google drive repository was organised thematically.

5. Once all the data was accessible, we individually coded for themes.

We then met and compared our themes for convergences and divergences as part of our meaning-making/interpretivist process. This process of meaning making was sometimes contested and always iterative before we agreed on common themes. The themes that emerged using this methodology is explicated in the section that follows.

Our work is therefore autobiographic since we reflected and wrote about our self-identities. The work is dialogic since we also engage in a dialogue between selves. This allows for the co-construction of meaning. Finally, our work is ethnographic since our research question is situated in the very particular culture of university teaching and learning during the Covid-19 pandemic.

The trustworthiness of our data collection and analyses is found in our work in three ways. First, we triangulated data from various sources (combined self-reflection, external data and experiential data). Second, we hold each other accountable in terms of coding and generation of data. Third, the themes discovered are related to a broader scholarly literature for contextual and theoretical meaning. Ethically we needed to have high levels of awareness of our accountability to each other and the project. Fourth, we had to be alert to implicating others in our individual and dialogical narratives. This framework for trustworthiness is supported by CAE experts such as Lapadat (2017) and Hernandez, Wambura Ngunjiri and Chang (2015).

Why is a Care Approach Necessary in the South African Context?

As academics engaged in social science research and teaching at one of South Africa's 26 public universities, we have both been impacted professionally by this crisis. Our discussion with each other via WhatsApp early on when news of the first positive cases of the coronavirus in South Africa first broke, focused on the stress around climbing infection rates in Europe, the fact that schools and religious organisations were still open, and anxiety around what the university response would be to this. Once universities began articulating their emergency contingency plans, we then reflected on the socio-economic contexts that staff and especially students found themselves in and discussed how this disease would find form in the different socio-economic contexts.

As we probed our understandings of the movement of this virus and attempted to locate the contingency plans of the universities within a society beleaguered by structural and socio-economic inequality, commonalities in our understanding and approach became evident. We realised that in the pursuit to find socially just solutions for teaching and learning, care and compassion had to foreground the responses. Viewing the emergency plans and quick pedagogical changes to online teaching through the dual lenses of citizens and teachers, we noted as Freire (1972) pointed out that teaching and learning are not only concerned with practice and methods but are also political and ethical processes. According to Freire (1972: 42) 'Political action on the side of the oppressed must be pedagogical action in the authentic sense of the word, hence, action with the oppressed'. Pedagogy then must take into account socio-political context of people in society and, as Veugelers (2017: 420) drawing on Freire (1972) notes, 'Education should support students in transformation and action for personal empowerment and help engender more human and equal relationships.'

Within the broad framework of care and compassion, our critical incident reports and WhatsApp messages revealed three broad areas around which most of our conversations revolved from the time news of the university shutdown was released. These include the lived experiences of staff, the lived experiences of students and online learning in the context of structural inequalities and decolonization debates. These will be discussed further in the following paragraphs.

Lived Experiences of Staff

We both established working from home as a normative work practice for ourselves. However, we soon realised that quarantine and lockdown conditions did not render this a typical 'work from home' environment. Our experiences in this regard were not unique. Other colleagues soon expressed concerns about the added responsibilities of parenting, caring for elderly and/or sick family members, home schooling of children, financial insecurity of spouses, inadequate housing, lack of access to family or friendship support networks and domestic responsibilities. The gendered nature of informal care for family members has also meant that women during the pandemic have predominantly adopted the roles of both caregiver and home school teacher. In a study conducted amongst 1,060 parents in the United States in May 2020, it was discovered that 70 per cent of home schooling was undertaken by women, and, among those couples who did not have an even distribution of labour before the pandemic, the absolute quantity of women's work and their relative share of family labour significantly increased, and '[o]f the mothers who continued to be primarily responsible for domestic work during the Covid-19 pandemic, roughly one-third increased their time spent in housework and care of children during the pandemic' (Carlson, Petts Pepin 2020; see also McKie 2020). These circumstances are not unique to the US, as globally the weight of caregiving is disproportionately borne by women (Robinson 2006). This, however, has multiplied under conditions of

61

lockdown and restrictions.

In addition to personal challenges, the pandemic also gave rise to myriad professional hurdles, which included the cancellation of an international conference, which we were both set to attend, and research projects being rescheduled. However, with instructions from management to be 'productive' during the lockdown the pressure to perform as teachers and researchers did not ease even during these crisis conditions. Academics have a dual role as employees in that they have to perform as effective teachers, which is assessed via performance management and student evaluations, as well as to present themselves, via publication as experts in their respective fields. Carrying the weight of this double burden during a crisis such as this, can be overwhelming, which we both experienced throughout this period. Our questions and discussions centred around how staff and students, women especially, could continue to perform effectively as teachers, supervisors, researchers and students while caregiving, home schooling and performing domestic duties, all during a global pandemic. This kind of pressure exacerbates what Currie and Eveline (2011: 537) describe as the 'long hours culture' with work bleeding into 'non labour time' (Cannizzo and Osbaldiston 2016: 890).

In discussing the effect of this pressure 'to perform' under these constraining conditions we reflected on how the new managerialism ethos, mentioned earlier, feeds expectations in academia and creates conflict between our responsibilities as social scientists which include our ability to meaningfully engage in activities designed to eliminate human oppression, and the corporatist neo-liberal imperatives of universities. This dissonance seemed even more pronounced during this crisis where we both saw ourselves, by fulfilling our duties as employees, becoming complicit in the reproduction of inequities in education and access to education. The kind of language which focuses on business continuity or business as usual contributes to the 'zombie' culture in the academy (Whelan, Walker and Moore 2013), and subliminally reinforces the mantra that academics 'should be doing more'. Ahern (2019: par. 2) argues that this kind of approach is '… increasingly commoditizing education and reducing the role of the student to consumers whilst simultaneously stripping the function and roles of our HEIs of their social, cultural and political meanings'.

It was this point that we questioned how an ethics of care and compassion could contribute to removing the management of uncertainty away from staff and students, and how self-care as opposed to productivity should be prioritised. In a study conducted by the University of Johannesburg and the Human Sciences Research Council (2020) among South African adults to determine the social and economic impacts of the coronavirus pandemic, it was discovered that the emotion most commonly experienced was stress

(57%), with depression being mentioned by 32%, sadness by 25% and only 13% described feeling 'frequently happy'. In this moment, where our human interactions with colleagues, students, extended family and friends are mediated by technology, how do we manage both home and work emotions and deal with what has become not so much working from home, but 'living at work' (Gwyther 2020)?

Lived Experiences of Students and Online Learning in the Context of Structural Inequalities

When using an ethics of care approach, emotions such as empathy and compassion are seen as essential to an ethical stance when viewing issues of access and inequality. This can then inform a socially just response to this crisis. For instance, while remote teaching plans were rapidly put in place in an effort to 'save' the semester, the reality that at the University of KwaZulu-Natal specifically, the majority of the students arrive from quintile 1–3 schools (which are non-fee-paying schools – located in the most impoverished areas in the country), did not appear to alter the course of action. Affected students live in precarious circumstances, such as informal settlements and rural areas without access to running water, and electricity, network connectivity, technology and data (which are essential for online learning). These pre-existing inequities in housing amongst students indicates that not all have a home environment conducive to learning. Students themselves have in newspaper reports, on online platforms and directly to lecturers expressed their concerns around these issues.

'Sorry my network connection is terribly bad,' she says. 'If it keeps on collapsing during a phone call, can you imagine what it does during internet connection?' Mtolo is a second-year law student at the University of KwaZulu-Natal, and is against the idea of online learning – the current plan for keeping universities working. Coming from Harding in KwaZulu-Natal, she says as someone from a 'deep, deep rural area' she knows that she will be at a disadvantage. 'The online learning will benefit the minority, who are privileged, and will not benefit the majority, who are poor, marginalised and who live in rural remote areas, like myself, with no network coverage. We will not survive it, we will not,' she said (Macupe 2020: pars. 1–4).

On 29 May 2020, the hashtag #UKZNisNotReady appeared on twitter, with students detailing their experiences, stating, 'The lecturers themselves are struggling to maintain order on zoom. Poor connection, counterproductive environments, there's a reason we chose contact learning instead of distance learning' (Ndumiso 2020); 'I live in a two-roomed house ... I live with my mom and 4 siblings ... my mom gives me duties for the whole day every day I don't have a place where I can study. Without being disturbed besides the students residence' (Zenande 2020); 'We are not against E learning, but all students should be given a fair chance to complete their academic year. No student should be left behind, resolve all the issues first. Providing data while we have connectivity issues is not a solution' (Luh 2020).[6] These tweets, amongst others, were posted just two days before online learning was set to begin at UKZN. In addition, students posted pictures showing the unfavourable environments they were in.

Apart from structural concerns, issues of gender-based violence and other forms of abuse have also been highlighted by students. In addition, black men and women in crowded townships are more likely to bear the brunt of police brutality for defying lockdown restrictions (Karrim 2020). Foreign students, in particular, face a dual marginality. As Wemyss and Yuval-Davis (2020: par. 1) argue, 'One of the most extreme form of inequalities that often seems to be overlooked is that between those of us who belong, who have citizenship status and claims of entitlement … and those who have no such claims and rights and who are abandoned to starve and/or locked down in detention camps and other forms of incarceration.' They argue further that 'grey zones – spaces outside the protection of contemporary states' have been created for social groupings such as international students (Wemyss and Yuval-Davis 2020: par. 2). These grey zones offer limited social protections and students face a lack of access to basic needs.

It is against this backdrop that students are undertaking online learning and also dealing with the scourge of Covid-19 which is ravaging the crowded townships in which some of them live, daily. For instance, in the first week of May 2020 new infections in the townships of Cape Town increased by 173%, due to lack of resources to isolate. As one resident stated, 'We don't have yards, it's one shack on top of the other. Our areas are dirty and smelly. This is the only place we have where we can sit and relax,' with another resident in KwaZulu-Natal's Umlazi E Section stating, 'We are not going to die from Covid-19, we are going to die from hunger.' (Jordan et al. 2020).

Increasingly the shape of the pandemic is mirroring apartheid geographies as seen in the Western Cape. For example, almost 12% of Covid-19 cases are in the black African township of Khayelithsa even though the township represents only 6% of the province's population (Al Jazeera 2020). In the days and months to come students will continue to be dealing with rising infections rates coupled with hunger and loss, and what this pandemic has surely revealed is a lack of care and community in the ways in which institutions have responded to this crisis. Strategies appear to be primarily grounded in a new managerial ethos which considers business over social justice imperatives. Less important are the multiple external pressures which include issues of insecurity, and the pre-existing inequities highlighted above. Similar critiques of universities and government were pointed out during the #RhodesMustFall and #FeesMustFall student movements in 2015 and 2016. Such rhetoric serves only to reproduce and preserve colonial and apartheid legacies that continue to exclude the majority black student body, and does not serve the larger transformation agenda.

Decolonisation Debates

Debates on decolonisation at South African universities have come into sharp focus in recent years. While strides are being made, an approach to teaching and learning, during the pandemic, that ignores colonial cultural capital among students will only perpetuate inequities already inherited from colonialism and apartheid and will also serve to devalue students' own knowledge (Maseko 2018). Paramount to decolonisation is to consider the lived experiences of students which can then inform socially just approaches to teaching and learning.

It is well known that decolonisation involves more than just changing the curriculum, therefore employing an approach that includes compassionate pedagogy can be used as part of the decolonial strategy which considers both the student and the teacher. Sykes and Gachago (2018: 83) argue that, 'One way to approach the project of decolonising the university is to employ decolonising pedagogies, which allow the whole of people's lived experience into teaching and learning spaces, affirm this experience as worthy of scholarly attention and create a dialogue between experience and theory.' As academics and teachers, we have to actively demonstrate our application of decolonising pedagogies as opposed to only curriculum transformation. As Vandeyar (2019: 2) argues, 'Academics are not merely conduits of the curriculum. They are complex beings constituted amongst other things of an identity, value systems, beliefs and lived experiences all of which inform their practice within particular contexts.'

In addition to acknowledging the teacher, Mbembe (2016) also emphasises decolonising systems of management. Much of our discussions during this period focused on how an ethics of care must include the decision-making structures of the university, which have increasingly come to include administrative officials meant to serve in 'support' of the primary function of the university. These officials, including human resource administrators, however are not expected to be proficient in the language of social justice pedagogy or to be involved in academic discussions concerning curriculum reform, transformation or decolonisation. The people furthest away from the students, are the ones who have the power to determine their futures, however these officials may not have the capacity to factor in the complexities of students' concerns. Transformation and decolonisation therefore cannot be reduced to key performance areas (KPA's) of new managerialist performance management systems. While great emphasis is placed on curriculum transformation during decolonisation discussions, we should be mindful of the architects of management practices and neo-liberal policies that undermine efforts for lasting change. These practices are then upheld along the management chain, resulting in academics executing policies, as employees, without an active contribution to the policy. For example, lecturers on the ground, the first point of contact with the students, are the last to find out when the semester will begin or end, or that they would have to implement continuous assessment for all modules both undergraduate and postgraduate, or that assessment would be halted until further notice. This universal approach to teaching and learning, especially during the pandemic does not consider holistically the teacher or the student in this scenario. Social scientists, whether teaching or managing, should not be complicit in the reproduction of toxic conditions within the discipline. Such an environment, based on a business model, thrives where compassion is non-existent. As Fox (1999: 24) argues, compassion is '… closely allied with justice-making, requires a critical consciousness … It implies a going out in search of authentic problems and workable solutions, born of deeper and deeper questions.' The emotion of compassion is thus critical to ethical practice. Noddings (1997) adds that social justice pedagogies are demonstrated only when teachers take into account their own positionality and knowledge as well as students' knowledge. It is only then that an inclusive and equitable learning environment can be produced.

While we realise that '[n]o amount of humanizing pedagogy and technology provision can remove the barriers and inhumanity of inequality' (John 2020: 2) given that online learning has now been adopted by universities in South Africa, how might this be implemented? Deacon (2012: 6) argues that 'creating a context of care is … even more pressing in online classes' than in contact teaching. How can academics respond to the 'zombification of the academy' (Whelan, Walker and Moore 2013), and how do we enact compassion as defined by Gilbert (2017), which is 'a sensitivity to suffering in self and others with a commitment to try to alleviate and prevent it'. In the next section we offer practical ways to engage with the questions posed here.

How Might an Ethics of Care and Compassionate Pedagogy be Practised by Academics in Higher Education?

Part of our strategic purpose in writing on compassionate pedagogical practices is to provide praxis for academics. By praxis, we refer to a set of actions that are an outcome of our critical self-reflection. In other words, they are empirically and theoretically informed sets of actions. We have distilled from our CAE work four strategies for praxis. We want to stress that sustained compassionate pedagogical practice is an outcome of sustained individual and collaborative critical reflection. What we are currently doing, as South African universities, is practising emergency remote teaching which is profoundly different from deep online teaching and learning. What is offered below is an outcome of our CAE since 12 March 2020. We believe that they can inform a sustained practice post emergency remote teaching.

Working 'with' Home

The pandemic has shifted conventional temporal and spatial ideas of work and home boundaries. Academic work has always consisted of a 'working from home' culture. The difference now, we argue, is that instead of working from home we are working 'with' home. The boundary between work and personal life is porous and there is no clear delineation between them. Childcare, home care, chores, lack of privacy, resources and lack of space all combine to shape the working with home experience. These may seem like obvious or 'common sense' assumptions of the challenges of working from home, yet our CAE shows that no acknowledgment of this was made by formal university structures. The plethora of communications from HR centred on mainstream managerial issues such as performance management and compliance with new Covid-19 legislation for example. Employee wellness is an outsourced initiative, with no congruence between the discourse of the private wellness provider and the official communication from the university HR division. Women academics experience the challenges of working with home more acutely than their male colleagues due to societally embedded ideas of gender roles. Where most leadership is male, this may often fail to translate into gender sensitive HR policy at universities. The concern of working 'with' home was taken seriously, however, when posed by students. Students claimed on social media and communications to the university (via the SRC) that they do not have conducive spaces for studying at their homes and that campus residences offer for most of them the only dedicated space with privacy and resources to study. The argument we make is that the working 'with' home phenomena is both a student and staff experience, yet there is no solidarity between these two groups on this issue. We foresee working with home being a normalised practice for the next few years in higher education. We encourage staff to prioritise the following when working 'with' home.

- Self-Care is paramount and, as Audrey Lorde (1988: 131) argues, it is a revolutionary act. In order for you to be present for your students, you need to be present for yourself. Once you have a sense of your own emotional, mental and physical safety, then you can offer compassion to students and colleagues. Mental health of both staff and students is emerging as an area of deep concern for mental health practitioners. As recent surveys have found, stress, anxiety and depression are increasing. The rates of these mental health diagnoses in people that have never experienced prior issues is especially high (World Health Organization 2020: par. 2).

- Boundary setting with colleagues and staff: The spatial and temporal shifts brought on by the pandemic have had many consequences for the way work is organised. Evidence shows that most employees are working significantly more during the pandemic (Kidwai 2020, par. 2) despite a concomitant rise in other time-demanding activities such as child and home care. As part of self-care practice there need be clear guidelines on when and how technologies can be used as work design tools. The both of us experienced staff WhatsApp groups and email communications that had no 'working hour' settings or other parameters. Staff were encouraged to form student WhatsApp groups as well, using personal devices. Again, similar lack of boundaries manifested here in both our experiences. It is important to communicate in a clear and respectful way what your time and other boundaries are regarding the use of technologies as a work tool.

Compassion is Leadership

Students will often look to you for leadership. A good leader during this time is one that practises compassion by:

- Being calm. The current pandemic is triggering immense anxiety. Leadership at the formal structures of the university may not be sufficient to calm students concerns. You will often be their first point of contact when it comes to checking in on the logistics of their courses for example. Your composure in communicating with students even if you do not have all the answers will assist them immensely in calming their own frame of mind. Expect to offer pastoral care as part of your role as lecturer and know when to refer onwards for professional counselling.

68

- Be open and transparent about what you know and do not know at this time.

- Recognise the disparities and inequalities that are being amplified during the pandemic.

- Recognise your own privileges at this moment and how this may unintentionally shape your interactions with students.

Advocate and Practise Compassionate Assessments

Assessments, their theory and practice have been a less visible part of the decolonial debate in South Africa. Most of the debate on curricula for example privileges discussion of content rather than a critique of the ways in which we continue to conduct assessments. This may be an ideal moment to rethink our assessment methodologies. Here we argue for two strategies:

- One is more immediate and practical. For example, as an outcome of our CAE work, we decided to advocate for pass/fail models of assessment rather than assigning grades to students. Students would submit a body of continual work over the semester for which they would get feedback. Based on whether they submitted all their work or not they would be granted a pass or fail grade. The policy was not supported with arguments against it invoking meritocracy. Instead, our respective schools are engaging in a mix of summative and formative assessments that really end up assessing students' access to Wi-Fi, safe working spaces and access to a range of resources from food to time.

- The second strategy is to begin critical self-reflection individually and collectively to reimagine what assessments would look like in the future. With the massification of the university, and classes in excess of 1,000 at first-year level in several disciplines, conventional assessments need rethinking. Students bring in their own cultural capital into the university, yet this is not considered as legitimate knowledge. For example, in Shaun's module, 'individual behaviour and organisations', he finds that students' already have rich and textured ideas and experiences of how workers (friends and family) have experienced work organisations. Yet this experiential knowledge of understanding individual and organisational knowledge is not leveraged. Whether we term these types of assessments innovative, critical or decolonial, it is clear that this period of pandemic may be an opportunity to finally upend the 'traditional' assessment methods we have been using for decades.

Trust: The Compassionate University

The compassionate university needs to become a long-term default setting. Universities need to shift away from new managerialism and micromanaging of academics. The claim that administrators are running the university is not a hyperbole anymore. At UKZN the percentage of academic staff fell by 12% whilst the percentage of administrative staff rose by 28% (News24 2020: par. 6). The management of academics has become professionalised. This managerial class is created and reproduced to manage academics. The pandemic is a period of organisational learning for both managers and academics. Despite remote working, technology has increased the monitoring and surveillance functions of academics by line managers. Work on organisational resilience globally and nationally is showing that trust and agility are key factors for organisational success during times of crisis. The praxis here is to engage transparently about trust with colleagues and line managers to advocate for managerial styles built on trust. We felt trust when colleagues, especially 'line managers' communicated with sympathy and empathy. This entailed acknowledging the challenges of working with home, the acute mental and emotional stress during this time and being validated as a human being rather than a human resource. Trust is also expressed through granting autonomy to highly skilled professionals like academics to act in the best interests of students and the university. The moments of least trust were felt during remote micromanagement practices. Cultivating trust is a process of organisational learning and needs to be practised at both macro and micro levels of interaction.

These strategies for praxis were generated through our CAE. Whilst they may seem common sense, as sociologists we have to use the lens of the sociological imagination to connect these personal experiences to a wider experience of higher education in South Africa during the current pandemic. Much of the debate is dominated by online teaching and learning and how academics have to retool and reimagine the classroom. Whilst we agree with these assessments, we also argue that managers of universities have to reimagine their roles. Key to this re-imagination is a rethinking the role of trust in organisations. We also find that the practices that need to change are also part of a larger decolonial debate in higher education. Assessment, university management style, self-care, compassionate leadership, managing people and students as relational beings instead of human resources are all ways of doing decoloniality.

Conclusion

This chapter through collaborative autoethnography has made three contributions. First, it extends the discussion of ethics of care to include decoloniality. It contends that decoloniality is an embodied practice as much as it is targeted at material changes to curricula. It also argues that an ethics of care and compassionate pedagogy has to be explicitly against new managerialist practice at public universities. Second, we show that collaborative autoethnography can be a useful way to engage with the lived experiences of academics. Through processes of collaborative critical reflection, it is possible to make visible private work and organisational cultures and our experiences of them. The purpose of this is to better theorise the social worlds we find ourselves embedded in, by applying a sociological imagination to everyday lived experience. This methodology necessitates a form of vulnerability that is often uncomfortable but needed to show how the narrative of the self/ selves is critical to understanding wider societal issues.

Third, we argue that employing compassionate pedagogical practices in teaching and learning are crucial to a socially just response to emergency remote learning. For academics, this involves imparting a culture of practice and community engagement, in addition to theorising. This response calls for critical self-reflection and an engaged academia that is responding in ways that consider both the societal and institutional context of students, relational leadership and a curriculum that caters for ethics of care. If we do not respond in these ways, deep learning and teaching will not be sustainable. Academic staff will become further disengaged, and a fracturing of the academic community will take place. Current debates on the survival of South African universities during this pandemic, therefore, need to elevate an ethics of care to the same level as that of financial sustainability.

The social sciences have historically led the charge on shifting towards more human-centred societal values. It is also the social sciences that can ultimately cultivate critical debate and provide practical responses to enable a change in the current policies that govern higher education institutions. For when the current coronavirus outbreak eventually disappears and the vocabulary of this pandemic is no longer in our language, how we responded to this tragedy, as academics, teachers, organisations and human beings is what will remain.

References

Ahern, S. (2019) 'Compassionate Pedagogy in Practice', UCL (blog), 3 July, https://blogs.ucl.ac.uk/digital-education/2019/07/03/compassionate-pedagogy-in-practice/.

Al Jazeera (2020) 'Coronavirus pandemic exposes South Africa's "brutal inequality"', https://www.aljazeera.com/news/2020/06/coronavirus-pandemic-exposes-south-africa-brutal-inequality-200612161408571.html.

Anderson, G. (2003) 'National liberation, neoliberalism, and educational change: The case of post-apartheid South Africa', *The Journal of African American History*, Vol. 88, No. 4, pp. 377–92.

Cannizzo, F. and Osbaldiston, N. (2016) 'Academic work/life balance: A brief quantitative analysis of the Australian experience', *Journal of Sociology*, No. 52, pp. 890–906.

Chang, H., Ngunjiri, F. and Hernandez K. 2016. *Collaborative autoethnography*. London: Routledge

Currie, J. and Eveline, J. (2011) 'E-technology and work/life balance for academics with young children', *Higher Education*, No. 62, pp. 533–550.

Deacon, A. (2012) 'Creating a context of care in the online classroom', *Journal of Faculty Development*, No. 26, pp. 5–12.

Ellis, C., Adams, C. and Bochner, A. (2011) 'Autoethnography: an overview', *Historical Social Research/Historische sozialforschung*, Vol. 12, No. 1, pp. 273–290.

Fox, M. (1999) *A Spirituality Named Compassion*, San Francisco: Bear and Co.

Freire, P. (1972) *Pedagogy of the Oppressed*, Harmondsworth: Penguin Books.

Gilbert, P. (2017) *Compassion: Concepts, Research and Applications*, London: Routledge.

Guterres, A. (2020) *Human Rights and COVID-19 Response and Recovery*, https://www.un.org/en/un-coronavirus-communications-team/we-are-all-together-human-rights-and-covid-19-response

Gwyther, Matthew (2020) *When Working From Home Became Living At Work*, https://jerichochambers.com/when-working-from-home-became-living-at-work/.

Hao, R. (2011) 'Critical compassionate pedagogy and the teacher's role in first-generation student success', *New Directions for Teaching and Learning*, No. 127, pp. 91–98.

Hernandez, K., Ngunjiri, F. W. and Chang, H. (2015) 'Exploiting the margins in higher education: A collaborative autoethnography of three foreign-born female faculty of color', *International Journal of Qualitative Studies in Education*, Vol. 28, No. 5, pp. 533–551

John, V. (2020) Fighting the Invisible Enemy, https://www.nihss.ac.za/sites/default/files/Covid%20Articles/fighting_the_invisible_enemy_-_covid-19_0.pdf.

Jordan, B., Nombembe, P., Pheto, B. and Singh, O. (2020) 'Nightmare comes true as Covid-19 tightens its grip on townships', *Times Live*, 4 May 2020, https://www.timeslive.co.za/news/south-africa/2020-05-04-nightmare-comes-true-as-covid-19-tightens-its-grip-on-townships/.

Karrim, A. (2020) 'Police Brutality: Why it's Easier for Cops and Soldiers to Target Poor, Black People', *News24*, 5 June 2020, https://www.news24.com/news24/SouthAfrica/News/analysis-police-brutality-why-its-easier-for-cops-and-soldiers-to-target-poor-black-people-20200605.

Kidwai, A. (2020) 'Covid 19 is causing employees to work longer and spend more time in meetings', https://www.hrdive.com/news/covid-19-is-causing-employees-to-work-longer-and-spend-more-time-in-meeting/576736/ www.hrdrive.com.

Kinnear, L. and Ruggunan, S. (2019) 'Applying duoethnography to position researcher identity in management research', *SA Journal of Human Resource Management*, Vol. 17, No. 1, pp. 1–10.

Lapadat, J. (2017) 'Ethics in autoethnography and collaborative autoethnography', *Qualitative Inquiry*, Vol. 23, No. 8, pp. 589–603.

Lorde, A. (1988) *A burst of light: Essays*, New York: Firebrand Books.

Luh, L. (@LuhLunganie) (2020) Twitter post, Twitter, 29 May 2020, https://twitter.com/LuhLunganie/status/1266330338835521537?s=20.

Macupe, B. (2020) 'Online push sets us up for failure', *Mail & Guardian*, 23 April 2020, https://mg.co.za/article/2020-04-23-online-push-sets-us-up-for-failure/.

Magoqwana, B, Qawekazi, M. and Tshoaedi, M. (2019) '"Forced to care" at the neoliberal university: Invisible labour as academic labour performed by black women academics in the South African university', *South African Review of Sociology*, Vol. 50, No. 3-4, pp. 6–21.

Maseko, P. (2018) 'Transformative praxis through critical consciousness: A conceptual exploration of a decolonial access with success agenda', *Educational Research for Social change*, No. 7, pp. 77–89.

Mbembe, A. (2016) 'Decolonizing the university: new directions', *Arts & Humanities in Higher Education*, No. 15, pp. 29–45.

Mckie, A. (2020) 'Juggling childcare with academia: female experiences in lockdown', https://www.timeshighereducation.com/news/juggling-childcare-academia-female-experiences-lockdown.

Ndumiso, A. (@asoh_ndumiso) (2020) Twitter post. Twitter, 29 May 2020, https://twitter.com/AsohNdumiso/status/1266293808934707202?s=20.

Noddings, N. (1997) *Philosophy of Education*, Oslo: Ad Notam Gyldendal.

Ntshoe, I., Higgs, P., Higgs, L. and Wolhuter, C. (2008) 'The changing academic profession in higher education and new managerialism and corporatism in South Africa', *South African Journal of Higher Education*, Vol. 22, No. 2, pp. 391–403.

News24.com (2020) 'Cash Crunch for Varsities', https://www.news24.com/news24/southafrica/news/cash-crunch-for-varsities-20200608.

Robinson, F. (2006) 'Beyond Labour Rights', *International Feminist Journal of Politics*, Vol. 8, No. 3, pp. 321–342.

Sewpersad, R., Ruggunan, S., Adam, J. and Krishna, S. (2019) 'The impact of the psychological contract on academics', *SAGE Open*, (April).

Sykes, P. and Gachago, D. (2018) 'Creating "safe-ish" learning spaces – attempts to practice an ethics of care', *South African Journal of Higher Education*, No. 6, pp. 83–98.

University of Johannesburg and Human Sciences Research Council (2020) 'UJ Coronavirus Impact Survey Summary Findings – April 2020', Johannesburg: University of Johannesburg, https://www.uj.ac.za/newandevents/Documents/UJ%20HSRC%20summary%20report%20v1.pdf.

Vandeyar, S. (2019) 'Why decolonising the South African university curriculum will fail', *Teaching in Higher Education*, https://doi.org/10.1080/13562517.2019.1592149.

Veugelers, W. (2017) 'The moral in Paulo Freire's educational work: What moral education can learn from Paulo Freire', *Journal of Moral Education*, No. 46, pp. 412–421.

Webster, E, and Mosoetsa S. (2002) 'At the chalk face: Managerialism and the changing academic workplace 1995–2001', *Transformation*, Vol. 48, No.4, pp. 59–82.

Weil, B. (2020) *The 'Good' Coronavirus Citizen, the 'Covidiot', and the Privilege of #stayathome*, https://discoversociety.org/2020/04/01/the-good-coronavirus-citizen-the-covidiot-and-the-privilege-of-stayathome/.

Wemyss, G. and Yuval-Davis, N. (2020) *Grey Zones in the Times of the COVID-19 Pandemic*, https://acssmigration.wordpress.com/2020/05/19/grey-zones-in-the-times-of-the-covid-19-pandemic/.

Whelan, A., Walker, R. and Moore, C. (eds) (2013) *Zombies in the Academy: Living Death in Higher Education*, Chicago: The University of Chicago Press.

World Health Organization (2020) 'Facing mental health fallout from the coronavirus pandemic', https://www.who.int/news-room/feature-stories/detail/facing-mental-health-fallout-from-the-coronavirus-pandemic.

Zenande (@Zenande89920416)) (2020) Twitter post, Twitter, 29 May 2020, https://twitter.com/Zenande89920416/status/1266293432114311169?s=20.

Endnotes

1 On 30 April 2020 the South African government announced the five stages of lockdown that the country would have to move through in order to ensure a safe phased re-opening of the economy. At stage five, all sectors of the economy that were not considered essential were shut down.

2 New managerialism is a form of management that prioritises product over process, engages in surveillance, monitoring and micro control of staff, uses the language and practices of the for-profit sector to shape university practices. For example, students become 'customers'. Efficiencies replace relational values. Financial controls are centralised to line managers. A managerial class is created to supervise non-management staff. Trends towards casualisation of staff are encouraged as a means of efficiency (Sewpersad et al. 2019).

3 There are a number of evolving dimensions of social justice in the humanities. For the purpose of this chapter we focus on two of them, i.e., ethics of care and pedagogy of compassion.

4 Several issues prompt student protests in South Africa, ranging from calls to transform the curriculum, to more equitable access to education (for example, more student funding, as well as access to safe and secure accommodation).

5 UKZN was formed in 2004 as a result of the merger between the University of Natal and the University of Durban-Westville.

6 These tweets are available on the public social media platform, Twitter, and are accessible without a twitter account.

Chapter 4

Rethinking Knowledge Production, Methodological and Theoretical Pragmatism during the Covid-19 Pandemic: The Case of Masters and Doctoral Student Supervision

Vivian Ojong and John Mhandu
University of KwaZulu-Natal

Introduction

This study was motivated by the need for postgraduate supervisors to adjust their supervision styles in response to the challenges posed by the Covid-19 pandemic and advise students accordingly. It draws from Bourdieu's treatise on habitus, capital and field to examine student supervision in the context of the Covid-19 crisis. Bourdieu (2000) maintains that institutions are regulated by internal rules, vocabulary and techniques. This is applicable to the context of this study; thus, it can be argued that students and supervisors relate and operate according to these sets of dispositions. Borrowing from Bourdieu and Wacquant (1992) and Huang (2019), these dispositions shape relationships of being in and out of a structure as it unfolds. In other words, these dispositions refer to the manner in which a thing is placed or arranged, especially in relation to other things. As moments and times unfold, they are always dependent on the conjecture of structure and action as evidenced by Covid-19. The Covid-19 pandemic called for high levels of flexibility in the manner people work with structure and action, that is, in terms of the structure of approval of a research proposal, ethical clearance, methodology, contracts between supervisors and supervisees, inter alia. As such, the current study argues that supervisors and supervisees ought to be conscious of this reality when faced with a pandemic of this magnitude and thus adjust their structure and action accordingly. The need to adjust to the dictates of the Covid-19 pandemic made this study revisit methodological and theoretical pragmatism. Thus, the study seeks to foster understanding of how knowledge can transform practice during a crisis, hence the need to re-visit the habitus, field and structure in line with situations imposed by Covid-19.

To slow down the spread of Covid-19, South Africa introduced strict protocols such as lockdowns, social distancing and curfews, thus necessitating a shift in data collection techniques employed by postgraduate students in institutions of higher learning. Restrictions imposed by social and physical distancing have forced postgraduate students from institutions of higher learning to conduct their research via online platforms. Consequently, both supervision and data collection ought to be done online in response to Covid-19 protocols. Methodological knowledge gained through the shift in data collection techniques was obtained from masters and doctoral students who had just completed fieldwork. The application of this paradigm is in direct response to the 'how' question of research and not the 'what' part as has been previously applied. Methodological pragmatism calls for flexibility in data collection techniques and must be applicable to research proposals, ethical clearance and contracts entered into by supervisors and supervisees. The main argument herein is that both supervisors and postgraduate supervisees from institutions of higher learning must approach knowledge production with new thinking and be ready to adjust to and navigate through the uncertainties accompanying the Covid-19 pandemic.

Objectives

1. To examine methodological knowledge gained through the shift in data collection techniques by masters and doctoral students in an institution of higher learning;

2. To re-visit Bourdieu's concepts of habitus, capital and field, and apply them to the context of methodological and theoretical pragmatism.

Theoretical Framework

The study draws on Pierre Bourdieu's (2000) theoretical concepts of the cultural capital, field and habitus. Bourdieu (2000) argues that cultural capital is achieved mainly via individuals' initial learning and how they are consciously or unconsciously influenced by the social world. Cultural capital is related to the resource of knowledge, most importantly how people understand the world. Bourdieu (2000) categorises capital into four elements, namely, social capital, cultural capital, economic capital and symbolic capital. Economic capital refers to constructed elements of production such as money, factories, buildings and property. Social capital is explained in terms of social networking and relationships among individuals. Webb, Schirato and Danaher (2002: 10), more accurately define social capital as a 'form of value associated with culturally authorised tastes, consumption patterns, attributes, skills, and awards. Within the field of education, for example, an academic degree constitutes cultural capital'.

Bourdieu (2000) conceptualises the habitus as a system of dispositions comprising actors that contain both structured and structuring structure. The concept suggests that social patterns and norms around actors are consciously or unconsciously created and adopted through daily life experiences. In this context, habitus makes sense when it is described in tandem with capital, field and practice (Huang 2019; Webb et al. 2002). The habitus reproduces both itself and its subjects through a production process that sustains a system of unequal power relations. By default, the habitus produces relations of control through institutions that distribute cultural capital in different ways among actors. This unequal distribution of cultural capital, as described by Bourdieu (2000), exacerbates unequal socio-cultural settings.

The habitus operates within the context of the fields. Swartz (2013) describes fields as power arenas; hence, it is important to understand the power relations within the fields that include politics, education and other social institutions where there is a visible struggle for power and positions. Bourdieu and Wacquant (1992: 16) stated that:

> A field consists of a set of objectives, historical relations between positions anchored in certain forms of power (or capital), while habitus consists of a set of historical relations 'deposited' within individual bodies in the form of mental and corporeal schemata of perception, appreciation, and action.

Apparently, fields represent arenas of production and exchange of services and knowledge. In the field, there is competition for positions that are held by social actors as they struggle to control different kinds of power, which Bourdieu (2000) refers to as capitals. Bourdieu's (2000) theory of the action is best explained by the concept of habitus and field, which seeks to show that actors develop strategies that are consciously or unconsciously adapted to social structures. The field of modern life also produces a precise complex of social relations wherein the actor engages in his or her daily practice where certain dispositions are developed through engagement with other fields that are operational within the same social world, thus constituting a system of dispositions. Simply put, habitus is to some extent reminiscent of the sociological concept of socialisation.

Methodology

The study utilised the qualitative research method and used the interpretivist research paradigm to interpret the meanings of the perspectives of the postgraduate students involved in the study. The interpretivist paradigm allows the researcher, participants and other actors to socially construct knowledge (Ponelis 2015; Mhandu 2020). The empirical material constituting this study was elicited from ten telephonic interviews conducted with five masters and five doctoral students from the School of Social Science, Howard College Campus. The researchers avoided physical contact with interviewees due to Covid-19 regulations. All the interviews were conducted when South Africa's Covid-19 Omricon cases were at their peak. Data saturation was reached on the eighth interview. However, the researchers conducted two more interviews for confirmation purposes.

The study used the snowball sampling technique which, according to Dragan and Isaic-Maniu (2013), is a non-probability recruitment method where the researcher uses a network of social connections to identify potential participants. This sampling method was used for it enhanced access to masters and doctoral students at the University of KwaZulu-Natal, School of Social Sciences. After the data collection process, the researchers conducted member checking to check the reliability and trustworthiness of the data. The researchers manually coded data and analysed them using thematic analysis. In line with recommendations made by Vaismoradi, Jacqueline, Hannele and Sherrill (2016), codes with common points were transformed into themes. Thematic analysis assisted the researchers to provide a rich and nuanced interpretation of the qualitative data. The researchers adhered to key ethical considerations namely autonomy, voluntary participation, confidentiality, anonymity and non-maleficence throughout the research process; hence, pseudonyms were used to protect participants' identities.

Setting the Context: Methodological and Theoretical Pragmatism

Pragmatism was developed in the late 19th and early 20th centuries as a philosophical and theoretical 'movement that focused on the practical consequences of social reality' (Kelly and Cordeiro 2020: 2). Historically, it can be traced back to academic scepticism which advocated for perfect truth. Kelly and Cordeiro (2020) noted that Charles Peirce, William James and John Dewey were the key proponents of the first wave of pragmatism (classical pragmatism). The entire human experience requires interpretation of knowledge and beliefs, which leads to novel ways of knowing and acting (Morgan 2014). Understanding inquiry, as well as interpretation of knowledge and beliefs, assists in providing a unique view of the social world. For Kelly and Cordeiro (2020: 3), pragmatism's epistemological stance ensures that 'the value and meaning of opinions and "facts" captured in research data are assessed through examination of their practical consequences'. This provides a possibility for a pluralistic view of multiple truths allowed by qualitative research.

Methodological and theoretical pragmatism focuses on the production of actionable knowledge, which is central in theory-informed research. It is an important research paradigm, as it provides a supervisory and guiding epistemological framework grounded in research realism and the entire inquiry process (Kelly and Cordeiro 2020). Epistemologically, methodological and theoretical pragmatism is anchored on the fact that research unveils the truth and reality by focusing on 'practical understandings' of real-world issues (Patton 2005: 153). Morgan (2014) concurs with the thoughtful ideas of Patton (2005) and adds that in academic research, methodological and theoretical pragmatism is compatible with qualitative-based interpretivist paradigm, which seeks to understand socially constructed realities by cross-examining the value and meaning of research data through examining their practical consequences. Pragmatism is important in knowledge production since it focuses on knowing and learning (Biesta 2010; Kelly and Cordeiro 2020). Essentially, knowing and learning are likely to transform practice. To this effect, pragmatism enables researchers to move beyond objectivist conceptualisations of realities commonly applicable in scientific research to explore the relationships between knowledge and action in particular contexts.

According to Kelly and Cordeiro (2020), methodological and theoretical pragmatism directs researchers towards making appropriate methodological and theoretical choices through unpacking pertinent research aspects at the design stage. Its characteristic focus on experience and action assists in refining research problems, theoretical framework and methodological inquiry, because the initial stage of the research process is often based on a practical understanding of the study and researchers often build on this scope to explore participants' experiences. Pragmatism allows researchers to overcome the contradiction between theory and action (McKenna, Richardson and Manroop 2011; Kelly and Cordeiro 2020) regardless of being criticised for putting greater emphasis on the practical component. It highlights the view that knowledge production is anchored on participants' experience, which inspires the researchers to analyse practices through experience and action. Precisely, a pragmatic approach to inquiry emphasises actionable knowledge, acknowledgment of the relationship between experience, knowing and acting.

Institutions of Higher Learning and Learning Shifting toward Online

Globally, institutes of higher learning have embraced online learning in response to the Covid-19 pandemic. Many countries closed institutions of higher learning, forcing a billion students across the world to shift to remote learning (Mhandu, Mahiya and Muzvidziwa 2021; Azzi-Huck and

Shmis 2020). Literature concurs that the Covid-19 pandemic has enhanced elearning, globally; Wisker et al. 2021; United Nations Education Scientific and Cultural Organization 2020).

Current projections in Europe show that Covid-19 has caused significant shock and severe socio-economic consequences to the global economy. The European Union estimated that the total economy of the European Union was likely to shrink by 8.3% in 2020 and 5.8% in 2021 and job losses were expected to rise to 10% (European Commission 2020a, 2020b). The effect of the Covid-19 pandemic is expected to vary across the globe, people, sectors and groups of students in institutions of higher learning (ILO 2020; JRC 2020). Also, technological development and climate change are most likely to have a transformative effect on how students from institutions of higher learning live, work and socialise (Centre for the New Economy and Society 2018). Elite institutions of higher learning with strong financial support and robust reputations are better able to withstand the impacts of the Covid-19 pandemic. The rest of the institutions are currently experiencing significant decreases in postgraduate students (Altbach and De Wit 2020).

As it explores the challenges posed by elearning, this chapter draws insights from Jappie (2020) who predicted that the transition to online teaching and learning by South African universities and institutions of higher learning would result in an academic disaster due to lack of internet connectivity and unavailability of gadgets such as laptops and smart phones (Jappie 2020). On the other hand, elearning during Covid-19 has played a vital role in transforming learning in institutions of higher learning. Literature confirms that elearning creates a productive platform where students can access a variety of teaching materials regardless of distance (Wisker et al. 2021; Hrastinski 2019; Mirriahi, Alonzo and Fox 2015).

Regardless of such developments, at the University of KwaZulu-Natal, where the current study was located, the majority of postgraduate students who participated in this study were either less privileged in terms of resources or they hailed from poor backgrounds. These students faced a myriad of academic challenges due to their underprivileged socio-economic backgrounds. This is also supported by USAF (2020) who argues that the majority of South African students live in circumstances that are not conducive for learning, especially at home where there are improper amenities and overcrowded homes. Extant literature shows that exploration of the challenges affecting supervision of postgraduate students in the context of Covid-19 has remained scant in contemporary scholarship. Therefore, the current study advocates the need for supervisors of postgraduate students to adjust to new styles of supervision that are compliant with the Covid-19-induced restrictions and thus advise students accordingly in response to these challenges. Times characterised by uncertainty require a hasty response to postgraduate supervision and knowledge production. As such, this chapter is a collaborative work that seeks to better understand the challenges posed by Covid-19 and how to navigate them.

Data Collection during Covid-19

The Covid-19 pandemic has changed the traditional ways of supervising masters and doctoral students. The key findings of this study indicate that lockdown regulations and social and physical distance measures imposed by the South African national government disrupted supervision of postgraduate students in several ways. The current chapter spotlights the supervision disruption experiences, challenges and lessons learned from the Covid-19 pandemic and the far-reaching effects of the pandemic on knowledge production and innovation. The recruitment of participants was one of the main challenges faced by masters and doctoral students during the data collection phase. This challenge is summarised in the extract below.

> The biggest challenge I experienced during the data collection process is the recruitment of participants. Working online presented challenges and I sometimes made appointments and the participants did not turn up or simply chose to ignore my calls. It took me several weeks to secure my first appointment after having called the participant for several times. My most recent potential participant turned the appointment down at the last minute. She ignored my calls and did not even make a simple apology. Some potential participants claimed that they experienced network and phone battery challenges. This was very frustrating. If I was to contact face-to-face interviews, it would be better because I would just visit her place. Also, telephone interviews were shorter than face-to-face interviews and this was due to airtime and participant fatigue (Masters Student 2, December 2021).
>
> As a doctoral student, I have a responsibility to contribute to the body of knowledge and scholarship. Even our proposal template is tested for originality and innovativeness in knowledge production. What I noted is that the knowledge production process is slowed by the online data collection process, as it is very hectic and sometimes you encounter a participant who cannot even use online platforms such as Zoom. I intended to conduct a focus group discussion via zoom, but I failed owing to such challenges. I found out that the majority of my participants were technophobic and hardly knew what Zoom was. I was dealing with elderly people residing in rural areas and I could not

expect them to be recruited online. Admittedly, telephone interviews might work but we cannot deny the fact that they are very inconvenient to such a population group. On cannot imagine an elderly person aged around 80 years sustaining on an hour-long telephone interview. It is a big challenge (Doctoral Student 1, December 2021).

The narratives cited above show that the recruitment of participants was a big challenge, thus hampering the online data collection process. An analysis of the two extracts indicates that the recruitment of participants took longer than expected; hence, it slowed down the knowledge production process. Although online data collection methods saved time by eliminating certain aspects of the research process, such as verbatim transcription of interviews, the researchers' inability to see participants' visual signals lessened understanding and appropriate prompting. The researcher's ability to prompt enhances the process of obtaining nuanced qualitative data. Also, participants' inability to use virtual platforms such as Zoom and Microsoft, as outlined by Doctoral Student 1, slowed down the data collection process. In addition to these challenges, one participant mentioned that:

Some of the interviews I conducted with participants were disturbed by participants' noise and activities. I remember encouraging one of my participants to go to a quiet place but he told me that he was at a taxi rank and could not leave the queue. I thought I was the only person facing this challenge but when I inquired with my friend who is also doing his doctoral studies at a certain university (name of the university is hidden for an ethical reason) he confirmed that he was facing the same challenges. So, many researchers are now conducting virtual and other forms of online interviews without consent forms signed by participants. This is unethical but the situation dictates that we do so (Masters Student 4, December 2021).

The narrative from Masters Student 4 shows that the question of privacy during the data collection process is difficult to adhere to when employing virtual data collection methods. The responsibility to ensure privacy is now placed on the research participant instead of the researcher. Also, sending back consent forms was one of the challenges mentioned by the participants of this study. They mentioned that some of their participants either took longer to send back the forms or did not send them back at all. This point was reiterated by Doctoral Student 2 who mentioned that:

I encountered many challenges obtaining the gatekeeper's letter and getting back the consent forms from my participants. I had sent the consent forms prior to telephone interviews and the participants were expected to send the forms back to me before the commencement of the interviews. I ended up conducting interviews without the signed consent forms, which contravenes the ethical norms of research. Only a few send me after the interviews but the rest did not send at all (Doctoral Student 2, December 2021).

The extract cited above shows that obtaining a gatekeeper's letter as an ethical requirement was a big challenge. Also, the research participants did not send back signed consent forms. These two challenges were so significant that they must not go unnoticed. In research, obtaining a gatekeeper's letter is an ethical dimension that must be carefully considered during the recruitment of participants. The gatekeeper's letter and voluntary informed consent must be considered and failure to do so compromises the reliability, trustworthiness and credibility of data. Researchers have an ethical responsibility to minimise anticipated and unanticipated risks, which include emotional distress, embarrassment, breach of confidentiality and ostracism. As mentioned by Doctoral Student 2, conducting interviews without signed consent forms contradicts ethical norms of research and puts gathered empirical evidence in disrepute. However, due to the challenges posed by remote and online data collection processes, masters and doctoral students choose this unethical route to circumvent the above-mentioned challenges.

Online Postgraduate Supervision

The Covid-19 pandemic has dictated that the supervision of masters and doctoral students be largely online and remote. Admittedly, there is evidence of remote postgraduate supervision in academic literature (Wisker et al. 2021; Nasiri and Mafakheri 2015). The current study confirms that evidence, as the results indicate that masters and doctoral students at the University of KwaZulu-Natal were used to contact supervision. Be that as it may, online and remote supervision brought a plethora of challenges and opportunities. Commenting on the transition to online supervision of masters and doctoral students, participants had this to say:

Supervision must equip a student with independent critical thinking and writing skills. What I have experienced is that online supervision does not allow supervisors to equip students with such skills. These skills are best transmitted through face-to-face interaction where the supervisor creates an enabling learning space to understand students' real stories and failures. Before the outbreak of the Covid-19 epidemic, my supervisor and I used to have meetings lasting between 2 and 3 hours. Now, the supervision meeting has been reduced to approximately 30 to 45 minutes as a way of saving data. Consequent to this development, students suffer the most. Online supervision saves time; however, I feel that students are no longer emotionally attached to their supervisors (Doctoral Student 3, December 2021).

Although online supervision compresses time and space, for me the new normal does not seem to work perfectly. I stay in a rural environment where network connectivity is a challenge, which disrupts most of our supervision meetings. The Covid-19 pandemic has turned our homes into learning spaces in spite of them not being conducive for learning. Although my supervisor sometimes tries to do her best to assist me, I strongly feel that online supervision alone does not give us enough room for interaction. Sometimes we end up communicating via WhatsApp using audios, but this too is insufficient for me. I prefer face-to-face and constant interaction with my supervisor. This allows me to express my emotions and thoughts, which is impossible via online platforms. I once suggested that we have at least one face-to-face meeting with my supervisor but due to Covid-19 protocols, my request was impractical (Masters Student 5, December 2021).

The extracts above show that remote supervision of masters and doctoral students at the University of KwaZulu-Natal has seen private homes being turned into digital learning spaces. However, this online initiative is significantly affected by poor network connection, especially for rural-based postgraduate students. Also, a closer analysis of the two narratives by Doctoral Student 3 and Masters Student 5 confirms the view that the Covid-19 pandemic has changed the landscape of postgraduate supervision. In terms of knowledge production, supervision entails supporting masters and doctoral students to gain knowledge, demonstrate dialogue and critical thinking and writing skills. This being the case, the two extracts above show that online and remote supervision does not equip masters and doctoral students with enough skills to develop independent critical thinking compared to contact supervision. Despite its advantages, such as compressing physical distance, time, space and cost, remote supervision of masters and doctoral students hardly offers students and supervisors enough time for face-to-face interaction, which allows the supervisor to gain a greater understanding of students' stories and real-world experiences. This finding confirms literature provided by Williamson and Williamson (2020), who vehemently opine that online and remote postgraduate supervision alone may obstruct the growth of the academic atmosphere except for concentrated efforts made by both supervisors and students.

In addition, Doctoral Student 3 indicated that online supervision hardly fosters emotional attachment between the student and the supervisor. The salient argument being advanced in this statement is that constant online postgraduate supervision is more likely to be associated with feelings of isolation and dissatisfaction. Furthermore, online supervision affects the interactive nature of the supervision process where students can share their emotions online. Significant levels of stress, loneliness and depression have been reported during the Covid-19 pandemic, as some students lost close family members. Failure to manage such emotional loss has drastically affected students' productivity. This analysis is complemented by Wisker et al. (2021) who argue that it is important for a supervisor to discuss the personal effects of the Covid-19 pandemic with students for them to understand their social and psychological effects which, if not managed, might affect their efficacy in terms of knowledge production. As such, supervisors of masters and doctoral students must prioritise the well-being of students even through online supervision to avert the feeling of loneliness and depression.

On the other hand, remote supervision of masters and doctoral students has benefited some students, especially the working class as they can work and study at the same time. In the case of recorded audios, students can re-listen to the audios, thus providing them with an opportunity to gain a more accurate understanding of the major ideas raised during the supervision meeting. Commenting on the importance of online supervision, one doctoral student recounted that:

> Remote supervision works better for me than contact supervision. I work 6 days a week, save for Sunday, which is my off-day and family time. We have supervision meetings with my supervisor via Zoom and we hold such meeting twice a month. My supervisor is very efficient and always sends me audio-recorded meetings via WhatsApp and I normally use them when effecting the necessary correction. I wish Covid-19 would have continued until I have finished my doctoral studies [laughing]. When I was doing my Masters, I struggled to have contact meetings with my supervisor, considering my busy schedule. For my doctoral studies, everything is working perfectly well and as I said, I prefer online or remote supervision to contact or face-to-face version. Online supervision allows me to work and study at the same time (Doctoral Student 1, December 2021).

The views of Doctoral Student 1 show that remote supervision plays a key role in sustaining knowledge production and is beneficial to working-class students. It allows students to enjoy flexibility and self-paced learning. In other words, online supervision allows students to grow professionally while studying. Receiving audio feedback provides supervisors and students with some in-depth engagement although the support of face-to-face interaction is required in most instances. The narratives of Doctoral Student 1 are contrary to the views of Bengetsen and Jensen (2015) who argue that remote feedback that lacks physical face-to-face audio interpretation makes it difficult for students to understand the recording thus slowing down the knowledge production process. However, central to the above extract is that postgraduate supervisors must spend more time managing the remote environment, have constant engagement with students and, most importantly, agree with them on supervision arrangements. These build trust and makes the supervisor–supervisee relationship much stronger. Postgraduate supervisors and students must embrace online supervision and collaborate in the production of new knowledge. This mutual understanding may enhance a supportive learning environment and a high degree of adaptability.

Conclusion

This chapter has unravelled the challenges posed by the Covid-19 pandemic in postgraduate supervision at the University of KwaZulu-Natal in South Africa. The study adopted a qualitative research methodology involving interviews conducted with selected masters and doctoral students from the School of Social Sciences at the University of KwaZulu-Natal. The study revealed two contending views regarding the methodological and theoretical pragmatism, and the overall agenda of knowledge production relating to postgraduate supervision in the context of the Covid-19 pandemic. The first and most popular view relates to the difficulties impeding online supervision. The outbreak of the Covid-19 pandemic and its subsequent and dramatic spread compelled universities in South Africa and other parts of the world to respond promptly and thus adjust their pedagogies to interactional online platforms. Research participants who shared this view argued that online platforms tended to occlude non-verbal channels such as body language and facial expressions, which are more explicit and easily understood during face-to-face interviews.

Anecdotal evidence unearthed by this study suggests that the online data collection method does not allow for a deeper view and nuanced exploration of participants' private lives. Just like other institutions of higher learning, the University of KwaZulu-Natal advised all students and supervisors to work remotely. Most postgraduate students who participated in this study are either resource-constrained or they come from poor backgrounds. These students face many academic challenges due to their underprivileged socio-economic background. The second view relates to how online or remote supervision benefits certain students, especially the working class. Online supervision provides flexibility in terms of time management for working-class students through self-paced learning, as it equally affords them the opportunity to sustain their jobs while studying. Surprisingly, this view has not been well considered by many scholars who have researched the shift to online pedagogies orchestrated by the Covid-19 pandemic.

Key findings from this study indicate that lockdown regulations and social and physical distance measures imposed by the South African national government disrupted postgraduate supervision in several ways. The current study spotlighted the disruption of conventional supervision as experienced by postgraduate students, the challenges faced and the lessons learned from the Covid-19 pandemic and the far-reaching effects the pandemic has had on knowledge production and innovation. Drawing on Bourdieu's treatise of cultural capital, habitus and field, this study has significantly noted that methodological and theoretical pragmatism is anchored on the fact that research reveals the truth and reality by focusing on 'practical understandings' of real-world issues.

References

Altbach, P. G. and De Wit, H. (2020) 'Post pandemic outlook for HE is bleakest for the poorest', *University World News*, 4 April, https://www.universityworldnews.com/post.php?story=20200402152914362 (accessed 23 December 2021).

Azzi-Huck, K. and Shmis, T. (2020) 'Managing the impact of COVID-19 on education systems around the world: How countries are preparing, coping, and planning for recovery', *World Bank Blogs*, p. 18.

Bengtsen, S. S. and Jensen, G. S. (2015) 'Online supervision at the university: A comparative study of supervision on student assignments face-to-face and online', *Tidsskriftet Læring Og Medier*, Vol. 8, No. 13, pp. 1–23, https://doi.org/10.7146/lom.v8i13.19381.

Biesta, G. (2010) 'Pragmatism and the philosophical foundations of mixed methods research', in A. Tashakkori and C. Teddlie (eds) *Sage Handbook of Mixed Methods in Social & Behavioural Sciences* (2nd ed) Thousand Oaks, CA: Sage, pp. 95–118.

Bourdieu, P., 2000. *Pascalian Meditations*. Polity Press, Oxford, UK.

Bourdieu, P. and Wacquant, L. J. (1992) *An Invitation to Reflexive Sociology*, Chicago: University of Chicago Press.

Centre for the New Economy and Society (2018) The future of jobs report 2018, Geneva: World Economic Forum, https://www3.weforum.org/maintenance/public.htm (accessed: 23 December 2021).

Dragan, I. M. and Isaic-Maniu, A. (2013) 'Snowball sampling completion', *Journal of Studies in Social Sciences*, Vol. 5, No. 2, pp. 160–177.

European Commission (2020a) EU Spring 2020 economic forecast: a deep and uneven recession, an uncertain recovery, https://ec.europa.eu/info/sites/info/files/economy-finance/ecfin_forecast_spring_2020_overview_en_0.pdf (accessed 19 December 2021).

European Commission (2020b) EU Summer 2020 economic forecast: an even deeper recession with wider divergences, https://ec.europa.eu/commission/%20presscorner/detail/en/ip_20_1269 (accessed: 19 December 2021).

Hrastinski, S. (2019) 'What do we mean by blended learning?', *Technology Trends Washington*, Vol. 63, No. 5, pp. 564–569.

Huang, X. (2019) 'Understanding Bourdieu-cultural capital and habitus', *Review of European Studies*, Vol. 11, No. 3, pp. 45–49.

ILO (2020) A policy framework for tackling the economic and social impact of the COVID-19 crisis, Policy Brief, Geneva: International Labour Organization, https://www.ilo.org/wcmsp5/groups/public/@dgreports/@dcomm/documents/briefingnote/%20wcms_745337.pdf, (accessed 23 December 2021).

Jappie, N. (2020) *Education researchers respond to the COVID-19 pandemic theme 8: Governance and management*, Johannesburg: Jet Education Service, https://www.jet.org.za/resources/theme-8_governance-management-in-higher-education-14-05-final.pdf/view (accessed 24 December 2021).

JRC (2020) The impact of COVID confinement measures on EU labour market, Science for Policy Briefs, May, https://ec.europa.eu/jrc/sites/jrcsh/files/jrc.120585_policy.brief_impact.of_.covid-19.on_.eu-labour.market.pdf (accessed: 23 December 2021).

Kelly, L. M. and Cordeiro, M. (2020) 'Three principles of pragmatism for research on organizational processes', *Methodological Innovations*, Vol. 13, No. 2, https://doi.org/10.1177/2059799120937242.

McKenna, S., Richardson, J. and Manroop, L. (2011) 'Alternative paradigms and the study and practice of performance management and evaluation', Human Resource Management Review, No. 21, pp.148–157.

Mhandu, J., Mahiya, I. T. and Muzvidziwa, E. (2021) 'The exclusionary character of remote teaching and learning during the COVID-19 pandemic. An exploration of the challenges faced by rural-based University of KwaZulu Natal students', *Cogent Social Sciences*, Vol. 7, No. 1, pp. 1–14.

Mirriahi, N., Alonzo, D. and Fox, B. (2015) 'A blended learning framework for curriculum design and professional development', *Research in Learning Technology*, Vol. 23, https://doi/10.3402/rit.v23.28451.

Morgan, D. (2014) *Integrating Qualitative and Quantitative Methods: A Pragmatic Approach*, Thousand Oaks, CA: Sage.

Nasiri, F. and Mafakheri, F. (2015) 'Postgraduate research supervision at a distance: A review of challenges and strategies, *Studies in Higher Education*, Vol. 40, No. 10, pp. 1962–1969, https://doi.org/10.1080/03075079.2014 .914906.

Patton, M. (2005) *Qualitative Research & Evaluation Methods* (4th ed.), Los Angeles, CA: Sage.

Ponelis, S. R. (2015) 'Using interpretive qualitative case studies for exploratory research in doctoral studies: A case of information systems research in small and medium enterprises', *International Journal of Doctoral Studies*, Vol. 10, No. 1, pp. 535–550.

Swartz, D. L. (2013) *Symbolic Power, Politics, and Intellectuals: The Political Sociology of Pierre Bourdieu*, Chicago: University of Chicago Press.

United Nations Education Scientific and Cultural Organization (2020) COVID-19 educational disruption and response, https://en.unesco.org/ covid19/educationresponse (accessed 12 June 2020).

USAF (2020) Business continuity in the face of COVID-19. Universities in South Africa. 1 April, https://www.usaf.ac.za/business-continuity-in-the-face-of-covid-19-dominates-the-agenda-of-the-usafboard-of-directors-meeting/ (accessed 23 December 2021).

Vaismoradi, M., Jones, J., Turunen, H. and Snelgrove, S. (2016) 'Theme development in qualitative content analysis and thematic analysis', *Journal of Nursing Education and Practice*, Vol. 6, No. 5, pp. 100–110, https://doi. org/10.5430/jnep.v6n5p100n (accessed 13 December 2021).

Webb, J., Schirato, T. and Danaher, G. (2002) *Understanding Bourdieu*, London: Sage.

Williamson, J. N. and Williamson, D. G. (eds) (2020) *Distance Counseling and Supervision: A Guide for Mental Health Clinicians*, New Jersey: John Wiley & Sons.

Wisker, G., McGinn, M. K., Bengtsen, S. S., Lokhtina, I., He, F., Cornér, S., Leshem, S., Inouye, K. and Löfström, E. (2021) 'Remote doctoral supervision experiences: Challenges and affordances', *Innovations in Education and Teaching International*, Vol. 58, No. 6, pp. 612–623.

Chapter 5

Elearning and Work Readiness – The (Unintended) Impact of Teaching Strategies in Response to Covid-19

Belinda Johnson
University of KwaZulu-Natal

Introduction

Prior to the first half of 2020, the adoption of elearning mechanisms in South African universities has been characterised by uneven patterns of development or adoption. However, the impact of the novel Coronavirus and forced social distancing has compelled the need for a rapid metamorphosis of teaching techniques in the tertiary education sector as opposed to a gradual evolution. The existing body of research on elearning in the academy suggests that there is a significant overlap in the skills acquired through elearning and those that also enhance graduate employability. In the past two decades, restructuring in the traditional tertiary education has seen a massification of student numbers, accompanied by a lowering of entrance requirements and a commodification of degrees. These developments have taken place in an era where there is also a renewed focus on the development of 'work ready' graduates. Questions concerning graduate attributes or issues of graduate work readiness necessitate revisiting and even challenging traditional teaching approaches, evaluating not only what should be taught, but how it is taught and for what purpose. Proponents of transformation of higher education argue that it needs to evolve to fit the requirements of a rapidly evolving employment sector in order to produce graduates whose attributes are the ability to think critically and who have the self-reflexive, lifelong learning skills that allow them to adapt to an environment where knowledge is in a constant state of flux, both growing and changing with the constant addition of new information in order to meet new job requirements. Tertiary institutions in South Africa have begun to explore new approaches in teaching and learning that are supposed to simultaneously adjust to the challenges posed by the changing characteristics of the student body as well as well as meeting the rapidly evolving requirements in the employment sector. One of the strategic approaches which are increasingly being adopted worldwide is teaching approaches that use elearning techniques. This research aims to assess the extent to which the elearning policies and strategies currently being adopted by the School of Social Sciences at the University of KwaZulu-Natal in response to the restrictions imposed by Covid 19, also affect graduate employability.

The theoretical framework informing this study is drawn from policy implementation and monitoring and evaluation. Developing or formulating policy approaches or strategies are supposed to be guided by the best evidence that is a product of existing evidence regarding the best practices. Current policy formulation and development in South Africa is supposed to be informed by the best existing practices and is supposed to be evidence based and results oriented. A key aspect that forms implementation research is to acknowledge that policy does not form in a vacuum. It is the product of and shaped by the milieu in which it emerges, and this affects the extent to which the main objectives and goals of the actual policy are shaped. At each step of the policy process a number of decisions or choices are made about the type of policy being designed, the type of resources being allocated to target beneficiaries, the degree of responsiveness of policy implementers (in this context, the staff and structures at the University of KwaZulu-Natal that are involved in and affected by elearning) and the degree of compliance from the student body itself, when adapting to remote and elearning imperatives and approaches. This chapter therefore looks at what factors and variables have influenced choices made about policy goals, strategies and instruments, and what the subsequent effect of this has been on the process of implementation.

On 5 March 2020, the National Institute of Communicable Diseases confirmed the first recorded case of Covid-19 and by 15 March, the President of South Africa, Cyril Ramaphosa had announced a national state of disaster in response to the possible spread of Covid-19. Within days the tertiary institutions in South Africa were beginning to plan ahead and develop a strategic approach that would mitigate the impact of the virus and its possible spread in South Africa in the 2020 academic year. UKZN had already cancelled the April 2020 graduation ceremony and at this point was in consultation with key stakeholders which included the World Health Organization Africa Regional Office (WHOAFRO), the National Institute for Communicable Diseases (NICD), the National Department of Health (NDH) and the strategic in-house experts at the UKZN, who had formed a task team to deal with the effect of Covid-19. On 17 March the Vice Chancellor announced the commencement of an early mid-term break. At this point, UKZN students were instructed to vacate residences by the 20th March and return home, and the majority of both the professional and academic staff were told to work remotely from home. Only staff deemed 'essential' to the functioning of the university were allowed to be present on campus.

The immediate point of any policy analysis needs to focus on the variables present that give rise to policy interventions. In the context of universities like the UKZN moving to adopt online and remote learning, the environment which produced and shaped the goals and objectives was one of immediate necessity and the need to introduce strategies that would allow the 2020 academic programme to be 'saved'. This disruption of the academic programme at the University of KwaZulu-Natal placed additional pressure on both staff and students since the academic programmes had already experienced considerable disruptions during the February/March period in the form of student protests which been initiated by the fact that students who owed fees to the university could register only if they had serviced 15% of their historical debt. The initial plan was for the university to resume the academic programme on 14 April, although whether this would mean the resumption of contact lectures or alternative teaching approaches such as remote learning or online lectures was still up for debate.

However, by the start of April 2020 it was already apparent that the resumption of the academic programme would not be a 'return to business as normal'. Over the mid-term break, the university had considered alternative strategic plans that would allow for the introduction of online learning and remote teaching. When assessing the interventions or projects designed to facilitate the elearning, remote learning and online teaching at the University of KwaZulu-Natal, it is also necessary to give attention to the historical environment. Prior to this period of time, the University of KwaZulu-Natal did not have an official elearning policy that informed its teaching approach. There was an elearning team that had been constituted for a number of years though, the membership of which was constituted by professional staff from ICS and academic staff from a number of the different colleges. Their ultimate objective was to explore the feasibility of different elearning approaches and strategies that the university could possibly adopt in the future in order to allow remote and online learning for a number of its qualifications. A number of academic members of this committee (especially those from education), who had piloted or were piloting elearning in different modules, were able to report back on mechanisms, strategies and resources needed in order to allow successful elearning to take place. However, the intention at the University of KwaZulu-Natal had never been to adopt elearning as the primary mode of instruction. The University of KwaZulu-Natal, like the majority of universities in South Africa, was primarily designed around the practice of contact learning and the curriculum in most of the colleges had been designed around this assumption. In addition to this, the University of KwaZulu-Natal's demographics had changed rapidly since the initial restructuring of the university in the post-2004 period. This period saw the amalgamation of the two former 'white' universities, the University of Natal, Pietermaritzburg, and the University of Natal, Durban, and a former 'black' university, the University of Durban-Westville.

It is also within the context of this merger and subsequent larger changes in the tertiary education sectors, both nationally and globally, that the advent and introduction of elearning must also be viewed.

Structural Changes and Transformation in the Academy: National and International Trends

In the early 2000, the tertiary education sector, globally, was undergoing various different transformation processes and the University of KwaZulu-Natal was not exempt from those changes. At the local level, and an amalgamation of three separate universities took place to form a new institution, the University of KwaZulu-Natal. In the post-apartheid period in South Africa, both the basic and higher education sector was evolving and in a state of flux as discriminatory practices and policies were being overhauled or discarded in order to facilitate and widen access to different race groups in South Africa and to address the needs of historically disadvantaged groups. By the early 2000s, not only was the transformation of universities being informed by local imperatives and demands, but by the intense restructuring of the tertiary education sector that was taking place globally. A second major trend that was also rapidly changing the manner in which universities operated was the commodification of qualifications, a process which began to increase the cost of studying at university. These two processes should theoretically be at odds with one another, with the influence of the latter having a substantial curtailing effect on the former, and would have done so had these processes not been accompanied by financial institutions offering more extensive financial support in the form of student loans or government grants. Another key global issue that was making itself felt on how universities operated in these conditions was that despite an increase in student fees and numbers, spending on the tertiary education sector was static or, in some cases, reduced as a result of budget cuts and fiscal restraints (Hornsby 2013).

This was unfortunately the budgetary trajectory that South Africa followed. Although both basic and higher education in South Africa has been undergoing transformation since 1994, to address the disadvantages perpetuated by the apartheid system, the current educational sectors are increasingly characterised by dysfunction by not providing adequate support for the effects of the changing demographic profile and massification. At the basic education level, the schooling system is still negatively affected and most public schools operate in perpetual crisis mode, with the result that students are left unprepared for university (Wilson-Strydom 2010). Although the lack of preparation is a global phenomenon and not unique to South Africa, the history of this country has exacerbated the problems that are experienced globally. Current approaches to bridge the gap between South Africa's ailing basic education sector and preparing students for university level education have included a range of mechanisms such as: foundation programmes, entrance tests and programmes being redesigned so that they offer more academic support to students who are struggling. Although some of these programmes have had individual success overall, student throughput is still poor.

The reduction of public spending on higher education and the limitation to further funding in the wake of substantially larger classes limited staff numbers and increased student enrolments. Unfortunately, these last two factors had an almost immediate and detrimental effect on the teaching experience in terms of quality, student performance and engagement as well as motivation and this began to undermine the key learning objectives of universities which was to facilitate the students' abilities to develop 'higher functioning cognitive skills including problem solving, critical learning, adaptability and lifelong learning' (Hornby 2013). Research conducted in South Africa over the past 20 years has identified that there are two different dimensions of access – formal and epistemological – when it comes to South African universities. Formal access, which has been increasing and subsequently improving equity has resulted in larger student numbers. Epistemological access, which influences students both throughput and their attainment of higher cognitive functioning through the development of necessary skills, must be supported so that large class numbers do not undermine the teaching quality and standards. This in turn means rethinking pedagogical approaches to develop more effective teaching strategies and accompanying the development of these approaches with investment in both educational infrastructure and human resources (CHE 2010). Current research focusing on student throughput unfortunately does reveal that the support desperately needed in the tertiary education sector in South Africa is either lacking or being reduced (Hornby 2013). Researchers have argued that too much focus has been placed on the eligibility criteria of students as opposed to trying to manage under-preparedness once students enter the university. Conley (2008) argues that there is a difference between eligibility and readinesss, and describes the following four facets to assess the gap key which are: (i) cognitive strategies, (ii) key content, (iii) academic behaviours, and (iv) contextual skills and awareness.

There is a need for current teaching pedagogies to be revisited and for transformative curricula to be developed. Assessments need to assess students in a way that then feeds into the manner in which curricula are designed and taught. Transformative curricula are not just those whose course content reflects the local and global content. They also acknowledge both the individual needs of the student and the dynamics of the classroom environment and how these necessitate new approaches to how knowledge and skills are shared in an enabling environment. The emphasis should therefore be on what is taught, how it is taught and to whom.

Transformation at South African Universities: Student Access, Throughput and Numbers

Although transformation at tertiary education institutions has been an ongoing process at South African universities since 2004, there is substantial evidence that the institutional, pedagogical and organisational culture of the academia in South Africa has been slow and uneven and that the current mode of teaching, research and learning does not cater to both the immediate and long-term needs of the current student demographic. South African tertiary institutions are currently facing a massification of students in higher education. This has resulted in an increased number of undergraduate and postgraduate students. Admission requirements to higher education institutions have been amended and the Department of Higher Education has stressed the need to intensify student throughput. Simultaneously public expenditure on higher education remains beneath inflation resulting in reduced funding and a limited staff complement left to deal with large classes. Current research generates the link amongst education and development in developing countries. There is a clear correlation between quality education and socio-economic development. A quality education is also associated with strong economic growth and higher income levels and from which society derives both private and public benefits from producing additional graduates, and this has resulted in increased government pressure to enrol an increasing number of students. At the undergraduate level, academics as a result face the challenge of teaching enormous classes and supervising a sizeable number of students. The rapid growth of the student body has not been accompanied by an increase of resources that would have mitigated the impact that larger student numbers have on the ability of the university to continue to function as normal (Hornsby 2013). In view of this, government policy directives have been to broaden access in the scarce skills areas and to increase student throughput. Only 16 per cent of high school students will attend tertiary educational institutions but, when it comes to the dropout rate, a cohort study conducted in 2014 showed that of the first-year students who were tested for proficiency in academic readiness, only 10% scored proficient, meaning that they could cope with regular mainstream courses, demonstrating that a significant number of first-year students were not prepared for university level study. Additionally, despite the attempt to provide systems of social support to new students at the first-year level, the dropout rates stand at 30% of students during their first year, a period during which two to three times more students drop out than at any other time; and only 44% of students will complete a three-year undergraduate degree (Wilson-Strydom 2010).

The argument has been made, therefore, that tertiary institutions in South Africa need to look to the experiences of first-year students as they move from secondary school to university, and the degree to which these experiences demonstrate readiness for university. A useful analogy to describe the current South African context comes as the 'Humpback Bridge', which was initially used to describe 25 years of experiences of students as they transitioned between primary school to secondary school in England and Wales. In that research educators were unable to see over the hump and therefore could only make limited attempts to prepare for the incoming cohort of students, because they were unable to determine the students' needs and readiness. Likewise, students could not anticipate and prepare for the demands at a new educational level because their view was impeded.

This is a very useful approach for describing the current state of South African tertiary education which is both out-dated and out-moded in terms of how it assesses students' needs and contributes to their readiness for a university education. It is a system of education premised on the existence of generational transfer of knowledge from parents to children that equips them for future life experience. Colonialism and apartheid both ruthlessly restricted the build-up of that knowledge, particularly with respect to black South Africans. The current first-generation university students cannot rely on the transfer of intergenerational knowledge from parents as to what to expect, and universities have a limited awareness on the preparedness of secondary school students to meet the demands of the university environment. The current institutional approach focuses too much on eligibility criteria and then trying to manage under-preparedness once students enter the university. Universities should be developing a better understanding of what, if any, preparation is done at the school level to help students overcome the hurdle of the 'humpback bridge'. This means not only being aware of factors such as a poor schooling background, under-preparedness for Higher Education (HE) studies, epistemological access through barriers, inadequate teaching and learning support, limited finances and socio-economic factors but transforming the teaching environment so that they can be accommodated and addressed.

This issue of university curriculum transformation also leads to questions on post-university employment prospects and whether universities are producing graduates with the skills, abilities and higher cognitive functioning that are required in the labour market. The focus on transforming the higher education system is not solely motivated by historical injustices and inequitable access. In developing countries, higher education is a key part of national development and student participation is a key objective in these countries. This is because of the link between economic development and the number of graduates produced. There is a connection between quality education and socio-economic development, health, empowerment and economic development, and this has resulted in increasing pressure on countries to enrol more graduates.

A high-quality education has a positive correlation with improved income levels and strong economic growth (Hornsby 2013). It is supposed to result in the development of skills, attitudes and abilities which are contributors to economic growth, such as essential literacy, numeracy, motivation and perseverance. The production of graduates results in both private and public benefits. The former sees improved employment prospects and incomes, along with the associated benefits on being able to make investments and money. The latter leads to better salaries for educated individuals, a larger tax base and an increased consumption of goods. The long-term benefits associated with higher education are better health, a longer life expectancy, improved productivity, enhanced innovation and knowledge transferal between graduates and non-graduates, the stimulation of entrepreneurship and the associated effect of increased job creation.

This issue of university curriculum transformation and whether universities are producing graduates with the skills, abilities and higher cognitive functioning that are required in the labour market is one that also that needs to be assessed in South Africa. A concern that has emerged at the global level, when it comes to tertiary education, is whether students from both undergraduate and postgraduate programmes, especially those from the humanities (Maharosoa and Hay 2001), are being prepared for the demands of a broader work environment, and whether undergraduate and postgraduate programmes are producing graduates who are work ready or developing graduate employability and are equipped with the necessary 'life long learning skills and professional skills' that allow them not only to find employment, but progress in their career (De la Harpe 2000). Issues of graduate work readiness or employability raise questions about what the function of tertiary institutions are, and challenges traditional notions of not just what should be taught in the classroom, but how it should be taught and for what purpose.

The relationship between higher education institutions, government and business is under a constant state of evolution characterised by debates about what the role is for tertiary institutions – providing an education or a workforce or both. Increasingly, governments and businesses are demanding that the academy moves beyond traditional approaches in the classroom and teach with the aim of enhancing employability. The massification of education, where over half of each generation now has the opportunity to enter tertiary institutions, has however resulted in graduates needing to acquire a broader range of skills, abilities and knowledge. This is because graduates are now expected to be prepared to find jobs in a wider range of areas. Employers also want graduate attributes that will allow their organisations to function effectively and efficiently, therefore graduates need to be flexible to changes in job requirements as well as being able to adapt to different careers.

In South Africa, higher education curricula reform has used the National Qualifications Framework (NQF) to try and erode the three sets of boundaries that exist between: (i) education and training; (ii) academic and everyday knowledge; and (iii) disciplines and subjects in the academic domain. It is hoped that this will result in the weakening of boundaries between social groups on the basis of race and social class and bring about an agenda for social justice. This should also allow for the modernisation of the higher education system, allow for greater mobility of learners allowing them to move between academic and vocational programmes and enhance graduate work readiness. The argument is made that there needs to be a move away from traditional curricula towards ones that promote inter-disciplinarity which are more relevant to the demands of the job market place and more responsive to local needs. Programmes should be designed to develop and enhance graduate employability, as well as developing employability skills and lifelong learning abilities. Employability is seen as a product of two dimensions. The first is concerned with whether graduates are equipped with the skills for jobs and are capable of being employed.

The latter focuses on job acquisition and the ability of graduates to find any employment. Graduate employability means producing graduates who are, therefore, able to acquire jobs, maintain employment and further their careers. Skills that are seen to enhance employability include the following four areas: traditional intellectual skills, personal attributes, key skills (such as communication skills) and organisational or institutional awareness or knowledge. Increasingly, the relationship between tertiary institutions, the public sector and the private sector are evolving, with employers and governments expecting higher education institutions to teach in a manner that fosters employability skills.

Online Learning and Graduate Employability

There is a growing body of research devoted to looking at curriculum transformation, remote and elearning and graduate 'work readiness and attributes' that suggests that a move to online learning in South Africa, which for the most part has been a reaction and response to the suspension of formal and traditional contact-style lectures, could also open further avenues to truly revise the pedagogical approaches to teaching and transform curriculum in a way that genuinely does enhance graduate employability. As a response to the enforced social distancing and temporary closure of tertiary education institutions, academics at UKZN are now having to revisit and revise their curricula in terms of skills outcomes of programme offerings.

While curriculum transformation and reviews have been part of an ongoing project at the University of KwaZulu-Natal for over 15 years, the current revising of module and programme content is being driven by the need to rationalise the type of skills development outcomes and applied competence that can be achieved in a limited period of time using delivery strategies (such as elearning) that most staff might be unfamiliar with.

Different countries have employed different strategies in terms of how employability has been built into higher education. Some countries use a first degree as evidence of employability while others have restructured programmes so that they incorporate features like workplace learning and the development of graduate attributes like higher cognitive skills and lifelong learning (Harvey and Bowers-Brown 2004 as cited by Cranmer 2006). Although different countries have different conceptions about what constitutes employability, there are common themes. In Canada and the USA, students' work-based and related criteria are assessed, whereas in Australia students must complete a set of 'generally expected' attributes (Cranmer 2006). Finland has skills integrated into both course and the students' own personal study plans, whereas in Denmark the completion of a competence profile is required by the qualifications framework. New Zealand, after consultation with education and industry specialists, incorporated specific measures into its own qualifications framework, and the National Qualifications Framework (NQF) in South Africa incorporates two sets of outcomes for the personal development of the graduate.

The National Qualifications Framework Act (No. 67 of 2008) allows for a development for an ascending ten-level framework, where each level sets out a learning achievement. One of the mechanisms intended to help facilitate the NQF objectives is what is known as Level Descriptors which are indicative of the broad agreement on the benefits of promoting lifelong learning. They provide a 'broad indication of the types of learning outcomes and assessment criteria that are appropriate to a qualification at that level' (SAQA, 2012) and informed by the NQF's philosophical underpinning with is 'applied competence', an approach that articulates with outcomes-based theoretical framework adopted by South Africa. The three essential components of competence are: (i) foundational competence which is the academic or intellectual skills of knowledge, the ability to analyse, synthesise and evaluate for information processing and problem solving; (ii) practical competence which includes the operational context; and (iii) reflexive competence as demonstrated by learner autonomy (SAQA 2012).

The NQF Act (No. 67 of 2008) allows for a development for an ascending ten-level framework, where each level sets out a learning achievement. One of the mechanisms intended to help facilitate the NQF objectives are what are known as Level Descriptors which are indicative of the broad agreement on the benefits of promoting lifelong learning. They provide a 'broad indication of the types of learning outcomes and assessment criteria that are appropriate to a qualification at that level' (SAQA 2012) and informed by the NQF's philosophical underpinning with is 'applied competence', an approach that articulates with outcomes-based theoretical framework adopted by South Africa. The three essential components of competence are: (i) foundational competence which is the academic or intellectual skills of knowledge, the ability to analyse, synthesise and evaluate for information processing and problem solving; (ii) practical competence which includes the operational context; and (iii) reflexive competence as demonstrated by learner autonomy (SAQA 2012).

Meaningful and responsive curriculum re-design will require not only the proposed foundational elements in the additional year to provide epistemological access to mainstream curricula, but should also involve curriculum enrichment through a review of curriculum content and breadth of coverage. This should be underpinned by a shift in pedagogy that privileges the attainment/cultivation of learning principles and the development of intellectual skills rather than the acquisition of discrete content knowledge. The curriculum reform process should result in radical curriculum enrichment with changes in structure, content and pedagogy that move beyond the remedial to the creation of conditions necessary for enhanced student learning with a view to 'increasing the number of graduates with attributes that are personally, professionally and socially valuable' (CHE Institutional Audits Directorate, Framework for Institutional Quality Enhancement in the Second Period of Quality Enhancement, p. 15). This ultimate outcome must require higher education to transcend structural reform and embrace the intellectual project of an emancipatory higher education that resists commodification.

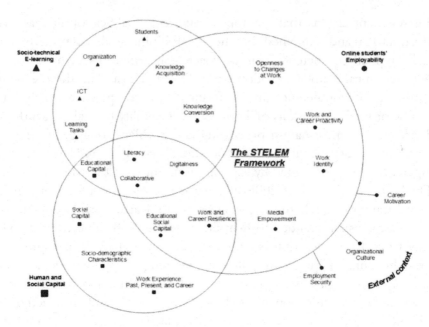

Figure 1: Model for the Socio-Technical E-learning Employability System of Measurement (STELEM) framework.

Figure 1 shows the Model for the Socio-Technical elearning Employability System of Measurement (STELEM) framework. This demonstrates that a socio-techno e-learning system which is constructed on terms of both social and technical subsystems also can affect student employability by enhancing skills such as literacy, digital collaboration, knowledge acquisition, dispositional resilience and adaptability and flexibility within the labour market. However, before one even gets to the point where it becomes relevant to determine what, if any, effect the revised curricula are able to have on work readiness and whether the delivery of these newly rationalised skills outcomes and competencies of students through the mechanism of remote or e-learning enhance graduate employability, the context in which remote or online learning strategies have been designed and developed, and the environment in which they are being delivered must be scrutinised. However, when considering the extent to which remote teaching and online learning will be able to service the current student body, it is important to constantly position any interventions in the context of existing challenges that are the ongoing reality that universities in South Africa face. However, this raises crucial questions when it comes to students and their performance and throughput, and how this is affected by their psychosocial and emotional well-being.

Any policy intervention that is going to be truly successful, needs to be well structured and planned and take into account any contingency variables that may disrupt the smooth process of implementation. Any form of curriculum transformation or change needs to be well planned and have clear measurable objectives and processes for realising them. While the revision of curriculum objectives, content and skills output using the mechanism of online teaching methods has allowed for the possibility of e-learning or multimodal teaching utilising remote strategies to be experienced and reviewed, the truth is that this approach has emerged as an immediate necessity to combat the potential effects of a lockdown and pandemic on the academic programme in South Africa. Curriculum design and development that will have lasting and contributing effects on the manner in which universities function and on the desired graduate attributes that are produced are those that need to be sustainable. And they are also those that need to be imminently suited to the needs of the students and the environment in which they study. Expecting compliance in the form of improved learning outcomes means that interventions are cognisant of those environmental factors that constitute the surroundings where learning takes place. Successful policy approaches in any field need ultimately to be able to cater for factors in the environment that affect a student's ability to learn.

Any change in terms of how the learning experience is structured and delivered needs to first start with how best to align the module content and delivery mechanisms with the local experience and knowledge of the student, while situating this in a position of relevance with the vast body of global knowledge. The discourse surrounding the latter should be one that views the global body of knowledge as comprising intertwined, different streams of knowledge in which no one stream should be regarded as exemplifying the objectives, norms, criteria and standards against which other streams' values are measured. Rather, the areas of contestation and articulation between the different streams should be emphasised. The transformation of curricula content cannot occur unless the assessments are done that identify the local forms of knowledge that inform the students' holistic experience and perspective. It also needs to be done while considering how its learning outcomes will capacitate the individual student in whatever environment serves as the classroom and this means understanding how different students from different backgrounds learn and engage with knowledge best. What has to be taken into account here is the needs of individual students and how best to engage with them using blended learning and innovative teaching approaches that allow them alternative ways of accessing knowledge, developing skills and becoming co-collaborators in their own learning experience, and how their own skills and knowledge can be incorporated into the classroom environment as part of the blended learning approach. Any change in the type of learning taking place must start with an assessment of how the students will adapt to the classroom environment that they are currently in, which necessitates detailed research so that the institution's approach can be informed by forecasting and projection. Remote learning where the 'classroom' is not traditionally what the student is used to does not necessarily reduce the quality of the educational experience. It just means that both the lecturer and student need to adopt more innovative learning approaches and strategies. Both teaching and assessments should therefore be able to determine what delivery mechanisms and learner strategies would best suit the individual students and these should be incorporated in both the classroom and into a personalised study plan for the student.

At the start of the 2020 academic year, the Minister for Higher Education indicated that over 50% of students enrolled in the entire education system came from poor or disadvantaged backgrounds. The National Student Financial Aid Scheme (NSFAS) serves as the prime source of funding for most students to cover basic living costs, accommodation and fees. The demographic characteristics of the average university student is poor, young, black and working class, who comes from a rural village or former township. The costs of stationery, meals and textbooks are settled by government for each of those students. The current student population at the University of KwaZulu-Natal is over 45,000. Seventy-eight per cent of these students receive NSFAS funding, which means that they come from a household that has an overall income that is less than R350,000 a year. Of the students who receive financial aid, 84.57% are African students, 55.46% of these are woman and 72.67% are undergraduates. Prior to the lockdown, UKZN had already been in a dubious financial position because of the amount that had been accruing due to unpaid fees. The protests that erupted at the start of 2020 were to a large extent motivated by the university's reluctance to waive the outstanding amount as well as its insistence that students pay a certain amount towards their outstanding fees. Between 2010 and 2020, the amount owed to UKZN had spiralled from R600 million to R1. 7 billion. The university representatives who were negotiating with the student representatives argued that the institution was simply not in a position to waive the amount owing in student debt.

UKZN's financial position was dealt a further blow when the lockdown restrictions took effect and it also became apparent that the situation would not be resolved quickly. The actions taken by the university to try and salvage the academic year also made it extremely obvious that the majority of students did not have an environment that was conducive to studying. A significant number of students did not have any type of device that would allow them to participate in remote learning sessions. This was particularly apparent when it came to the postgraduate students who relied on access to the LANs in order to complete their work. The majority of tertiary institutions arranged to have laptops and data provided to students. However, what had not been taken into account was whether the coverage and connectivity in the areas where students were staying was of a sufficient strength or quality to allow them to be able to attend lectures or seminars using Zoom or Skype. Although smartphone penetration in South Africa is relatively high, this does not necessarily mean that students are able to easily connect to the internet or partake in online learning. Just over 65% of South Africans reside in a household were there is at least one smartphone or other type of mobile device.

However, only about one million South Africans have stable internet access using fixed lines (APC 2017). Just over 50% of smartphone owners use them primarily for communication or to access social media. The extent and quality of their service providers vary considerably depending on the location (APC 2017).

Conclusion

When, it comes to looking at whether these students can be serviced via online learning or remote teaching a number of challenges arise. Within the first few days of attempting to offer online lectures or seminars, it became apparent quite rapidly that a significant number of students resided in areas where coverage was poor. Most students come from areas and homes where both the necessary infrastructure and learning contexts are inadequate and which will probably impact negatively on their ability to learn. Although the majority of universities may well be able to utilise the technology teaching practices that allow for remote, distance or online learning, the reality is that student access to and use of these require them to be physically present in an environment where they are available, in other words, residing on or near university campuses. The majority of universities also still function and are prepared for contact and face-to-face learning as well, where students live within commuting range of the universities.

Even the most innovative curricula transformation in response to the 'lockdown' cannot address the 'digital divide' that exists in South Africa and, therefore, the majority of attempts to address this will still be highly contested and linked to structures of power and privilege. While Covid-19 might have spurred universities to explore and adopt online and remote learning, it has also made access to higher education even less obtainable to the few students who were able to access it before.

Beyond the infrastructure, and the technological barriers to remote/online learning, there also needs to be an acknowledgement that the Covid-19 lockdown is an abnormal environment that will undoubtedly affect the psychosocial aspects of students.

References

APC, 'Perspectives on universal free access to online information in South Africa: Free public wi-fi and zero-rated content', September 2017, accessible https://www.apc.org/en/pubs/perspectives-universal-free-access-online-information-south-africa-free-public-wi-fi-and-zero. Byrne and Flood, 2005. A study of accounting students' motives, expectations and preparedness for higher education. Journal of Further and Higher Education, 29 (2) (2005), pp. 111-12

Cranmer, S. (2006) Enhancing graduate employability: best intentions and mixed outcomes, Studies in Higher Education, 31:2, 169-184, DOI:10.1080/03075070600572041

Coopers & Lybrand. (1998) Skills development in Higher Education. Report for CVCP/DfEE/HEQE, November, London: Committee of Vice-Chancellors and Principals of the universities of the UK (CVCP).

de la Harpe, B., Radloff, A. & Wyber, J. (2000) Quality and generic (professional) skills. Quality in Higher Education. 6 (3) 231-243

Du Plessis, L. & Gerber, D. (2012) The academic preparedness of students – an exploratory study. The Journal for Transdisciplinary Research in Southern Africa. 8(1), 81-94.

Enselin, P. (2006). Democracy, social justice and education: Feminist strategies in a globalising world. Educational Philosophy and Theory, 38(1), 57-61.

De Sousa Santos, B. (2014). Epistemologies of the South: Justice against epistemicide. Boulder, USA:Paradigm Publishers.

Gower, P. (2009, June 31). Idle Minds, Social Time Bomb. Mail and Guardian: Accessed from: https://mg.co.za/article/2009-07-31-idle-minds-social-time-bomb. 28 June 2017

Hornsby, David 2013.Teaching Large Classes in Higher Education: Challenges and Opportunities in a Developing Context. Canadian International Education Conference, Hart House, University of Toronto, Canada.

Lange, Lis (2010). Preface. Higher Education Monitor: Learning Beyond Formal Access. Council for Higher Education.

Lombard, Antoinette. (2018. "E-literacy massification challenges for rural and disadvantaged communities in South Africa," Proceedings of International Academic Conferences 7309974, International Institute of Social and Economic Sciences

Lulat, Y. G. M. (2003). The development of higher education in Africa: A historical survey, in Teferra, D. and Altbach, P. G. (eds.), African Higher Education: An International Reference Handbook. Bloomington: Indiana University Press, 15–31.

Malada, B. (2010, September 19). We ignore proper education at our peril. *Sunday Tribune*, 22.

Maharasoa, M & Hay, D. (2001) Higher education and graduate employment in South Africa. Quality in Higher Education, 7 (2) 139-147

Mbembe, A (2012). At the Centre of the Knot. Social Dynamics, 38, 8-14. 3. 8. 4

Morley, L. (2001) Producing New Workers: quality, equality and employability in higher education. Quality in Higher Education, 7 (2) 131-138Lees. D. (2002) Graduate Employability – Literature Review. LTSN Generic centre. University of Exeter. http://www.palatine.ac.uk/files/emp/1233.pdf Accessed: 27 June 2017

Mngomezulu B.R. & Maposa M.T. (2017). The challenges facing academic scholarship in Africa. In: Cross M. & Ndofirepi A. (eds.) Knowledge and change in African universities. African Higher Education: Developments and Perspectives. Rotterdam, Netherlands: Sense Publishers

Morrow, W. 2007. Learning to teach in South Africa. Cape Town: HSRC Press.

Nel, C. & Kistner, L. (2009). The national senior certificate: Implications for access to higher education. South African Journal of Higher Education, 23(5), 953-973.

REPUBLIC OF SOUTH AFRICA. 2008. National Qualifications Framework Act, No 67 of 2008. Government Gazette No 31909. Pretoria: Government Printer.

South African Qualifications Authority (SAQA). 2012. Level Descriptors for the South African National Qualifications Framework. Pretoria: SAQA.

Teferra, D., & Altbach, P. G. (2004). African Higher Education: Challenges for the 21st Century. Higher Education, 47(1), 21-50. http://dx.doi. org/10.1023/B:HIGH.0000009822.49980.30

UKZN@ a Glance (2017). Publications Unit

Corporate Relations Division, Retrieved from https://ukzn.ac.za/wp-content/uploads/

Wilson, M. & Scalise, K. (2006). Assessment to improve learning in higher education: The BEAR assessment system. Higher Education, 52, 635-663.

Wilson-Strydom, M. (2010). Traversing the chasm from school to university in South Africa: A student perspective. Tertiary Education and Management, 16:4, 313-325.

Chapter 6

Uncertainty in the Time of Covid-19: Attempting to Navigate Professional and Personal Challenges in an Institution of Higher Learning

Noel Chellan
University of KwaZulu-Natal

Introduction

At the time of writing this chapter a professor from the province of KwaZulu-Natal had died because of Covid-19. The academic was involved in the fight against another virus that has decimated communities in many parts of the world and more so in South Africa viz. HIV/AIDS. There are many others like her that have succumbed to Covid-19 whilst on the frontline of their work. Since then, the number of affected and dead in South Africa (SA) has risen tremendously. The number of infected people in SA as of 24 June 2020 was 106,108. Two thousand and twelve people had died from Covid-19 (MOH – SA 2020). Whilst sickness and death seem to be all around us and anxiety and depression hangs in the air, the various institutions, bodies and organisations in society are determined to continue with their 'normal' mandates. Whilst a university does have much more flexibility than other institutions in society, it too has its challenges in so far as attempting to find new ways of fulfilling its mandate as a higher learning institution. It is an enormous challenge to teach a module like sociology that has 1,600 students registered at the first-year level. The biggest challenge envisaged by me as a teacher is in the sphere of assessments, which is a fundamental requirement for the grading of students, both at the end of the semester as well as at the end of the year. Covid-19 has definitely thrown society into unchartered waters and the great challenge for us at both the personal as well as the professional level is to try and navigate this unknown and somewhat frightening territory: 'the Covid-19 pandemic has necessitated a national lockdown for at least three weeks and this has placed the operations of the institution in a perilous position' (UKZN Teaching and Learning Framework 2020: 1).

As far as I can remember, sociology at the University of KwaZulu-Natal has always had large numbers of students enrolling for modules in comparison with other disciplines. With the opening up of the educational system in South Africa and more support being given to historically disadvantaged individuals, the university has seen its student numbers grow rapidly. Sociology attracts large numbers of students at the first-year level. This phenomenon has its roots in the history of the sociology department, the thinking at that time being that lawyers, nurses, engineers and others should understand the type of society that they will live and work in. The intention behind such thinking was noble and well meaning. Hence students from many different disciplines would enrol for the first-year sociology module. Most students would end up doing it as an elective and not as a major, supposedly for reasons that have to do with vocational opportunities or lack thereof. Other disciplines such as environmental sciences, psychology, development studies and law tend to provide more opportunities in the labour market, but not sociology as a specific vocation. Austerity measures implemented at the university over the years also meant fewer teachers, larger number of students in the lecture halls, fewer tutors and less administrative support. Teaching in large classes dilutes the quality of interaction between teacher and students, although one continues to try and balance interaction with that of content delivery. Covid-19 it seems, provides both challenges and opportunities for how the university should or could function in the area of teaching, learning and assessment.

Covid-19 Changes Everything – Planning for Uncertain Times

The number has been rising rapidly since President Ramaphosa's first announcement. But we might be missing asymptomatic cases and other unreported cases. It is important for the world to be in lockdown and for people to isolate themselves, because this is the only way to break the cycle of transmission and replication of the virus. The virus is an obligate parasite: it needs a susceptible living being in order to replicate – the cell makes several copies of the same virus. But, if it cannot find a susceptible host, it will not be able to replicate and will become inactive. If people are not close to each other, the virus will not be able to be transmitted from one person to the next, and it will therefore become inactive. (Dr Prudence Kayoka, Department of Agriculture and Animal Health, Unisa).

Who would have thought that a virus would disrupt the functioning of the university in the way that it has! We are used to student protests disrupting the university curriculum and calendar, especially at the beginning of the year. When student protests have occurred, we have always found a way to work through the challenges of teaching and learning at the university, in general, and in the department of sociology, in particular, but Covid-19 changes everything! And so, as a teacher, I have more questions than answers. Some of these questions are: how do I teach in the time of a lockdown, how do I teach 1,600 students using the medium of remote teaching – a concept that I have only come to learn during Covid-19, how do I assess the work of 1,600 students, how effective is the technology in enabling the continuation and completion of the academic year, how does one get students to meet one half-way, how does one deal with students that have been excluded from the teaching and learning process for one reason or another, how does one deal with students who will use the case of non-contact teaching and learning to 'demand' that they pass at the end of the year, this within the context of students in South Africa having developed a culture of entitlement? Teachers are required to attend workshops on online teaching, a task that leaves many anxious as this means moving away from the conventional and safe method of teaching face to face in the classroom. The situation is, in effect, demanding of teachers and supervisors to be familiar with the use of all types of technology. We are being forced out of our comfort zones from what we know best. The university has undergone many forms of transformations since it was an apartheid institution but this calls for a transformation never imagined before!

But the Covid-19 pandemic may also provide an opportunity in the field of teaching and learning as well. There have been many discussions and workshops on pedagogy to get students to become independent learners viz. learners for life. With the appropriate framework and some careful planning, Covid-19 may provide an opportunity to explore methods of moving students away from being 'spoon fed' at the university level, to gradually shifting them onto a path of independent learning. This could also prepare them well for postgraduate studies, when a student is really expected to be an independent learner, but with adequate guidance from the supervisor. Most importantly, it may spur on students to becoming learners for life. Attending online workshops has also meant a refreshing and updating of one's teaching and learning pedagogies and practices. New ways of assessing and measuring student learning are being explored. But these are not without their practical challenges. Most academics are in the early or conceptual stages of attempting to transition from the physical realm of teaching and learning to a virtual one. However, the most daunting of challenges is that of the socio-economic context that characterises South African society and the majority of students who have to negotiate and confront such challenges on a daily basis.

The Socio-economic Context of Education in South Africa

Many have come to the realisation that transitioning to remote teaching and learning is not only a technological issue but a socio-economic one as well. In other words, like all things South African, the skewed economic development of South Africa has to be factored into any move to institute remote teaching and learning at the university level. South Africa is a troubled country with unique challenges. It is the last country on the African continent to have acquired democracy. But 26 years plus into democracy, it is still faced with huge challenges – the big three being that of inequality, unemployment and poverty. Prior to 1994 black South Africans were in the main excluded from accessing higher education. This stemmed from the racist thinking of the psychologist and grand architect of apartheid – Professor Hendrik Verwoerd:

> The Bantu Education Act was passed in 1953, five years after the National Party, under Verwoerdian control came to power. It was designed with only one purpose in view, namely, to deprive the most vulnerable sector of the population—the African child of obtaining a modern, free, and enlightened education (Gool 1966: 1).

So, for most of their lives, blacks would, in the main, serve as labourers and many would belong to the 'reserve army of labour'. Though moving at a snail's pace, that would soon change under an ANC-led government. Since the advent of democracy in 1994, formal education was made more accessible to black students. But the journey thus far towards accessing higher education has not been without continuing challenges. A key challenge was the issue of affordability or the lack thereof. This culminated in the violent student protests of 2016 which saw universities in South Africa undergoing their most challenging test since the birth of democracy. As always in South Africa, the student protests of 2016 were tinged with political influence and interference. The end result of the ongoing protests, as well as the factional politics within the ANC, was to witness the government subsidising higher education for students whose household incomes were below a certain threshold. This was beneficial for students, in general, and for black students, in particular. But we in South Africa know that with the commencement of the university year, we will not be surprised by any form of student protest disrupting the university curriculum and calendar. At the beginning of 2020, Covid-19 would not only force change from the perspectives of management and staff but from the perspectives of students as well. The university would have had to rethink its methods of operations towards a future that it is not used to, and this always means factoring in the views of students.

As universities throughout the country grapple with how to continue and complete the academic calendar in the context of Covid-19, student voices are already being heard on national media regarding their concerns, anxieties, requests and demands related to online teaching and learning. There is a vocal and militant student constituency in South Africa. The Student Representative Council (SRC) at the university is a powerful voice advocating on behalf of the student constituency. Each year it is not unusual for the Duly Performed (DP) criteria to be waived in some disciplines, as a result of SRC negotiations, and sometimes as demands. Hence in terms of student requests and demands, students have plenty of agency and they are represented by the SRC at the lowest, as well as at the highest structures of the university. The most recent request was for students to be allowed to go back to the university residences during the time of lockdown. The thinking was that learning could be more fruitful at the university residence. Notwithstanding what one may sometimes see as entitlement demands by students, the legacy of colonialism and apartheid is still very much part of South African society. The new democratic dispensation of 1994 in South Africa witnessed the commencement of policies and programmes to address the legacies of colonialism and apartheid. Whilst there is no disputing the fact that such legacies are far from being meaningfully addressed, the conditions of some blacks are relatively much better under the new democratic dispensation than they were under colonialism and apartheid. For the majority of South Africa's peoples, socio-economic conditions are less than satisfactory. A survey (UKZN Student online survey 2020) conducted during the lockdown 'to determine the level of technological access, literacy and preparedness of students' registered in the School of Social Sciences indicated that about 53% were residing in the university residences before the lockdown, about 28% were in private accommodation and about 19% were living with their families. During the lockdown – about 98% were living with their families. More than 60% indicated that they have 10 or more family members living in the same household. About 42% of the students indicated that they live in a rural residential area, about 30% in a semi-rural area and about 18% stated that they live in an urban residential area. A large majority (83%) indicated that there are various distractions at their work/study spaces at home. About 65% of the respondents indicated that any internet connections range from 'somewhat reliable' to 'not at all reliable'. There are other challenges such as types of devices and skill levels of technology use. With such feedback, the university has rightly conducted a dry-run in order to ascertain the level of preparedness for a transition to remote teaching and learning. The main motto guiding the university and correctly so, is 'leave no student behind'.

Ever since technology in the form of internet and email have entered academia, university life took small steps towards forms of remote functioning, especially in the spheres of administration and communication. Teaching and learning were never meant to be part of the online world. The default position was always that of physical presence within the premises of the university. That changed with the advent of Covid-19. The 2016 student protests and the 2020 coronavirus pandemic are phenomena that have made the university seriously consider carrying out its mandate and core functions using the method of remote learning and teaching, viz., that processes should proceed through the medium of technology. However, in a country like South Africa, where two of its defining characteristics are inequality and a culture of entitlement amongst certain sections of the student population, remote functioning is difficult for a university. As the university grapples to function within the context of Covid-19, it is becoming increasingly clear that it is not an easy task to transition from on-site teaching and learning to online teaching and learning, given the huge inequalities and lack of proper digital infrastructure for the vast majority of South Africa's students. Like so much of South Africa's history, with all of the planning and policies, students are bound to be left behind. Our history has shown us that when this happens, the situation becomes exacerbated. As a teacher under these circumstances and with the relevant support, one has to find ways and means to 'save the academic year'. It is then that the motto 'leave no student behind' becomes even more challenging to realise, but one that has to be steadfastly aspired to.

Navigating the Transition to Remote Teaching and Learning

> University systems have changed profoundly in the last 10 years. Larger and more diverse student populations, a growing interest in professional education and lifelong learning, the privatisation of higher education, financial constraints, enhanced attention to quality and accountability, and evolving tendencies for postsecondary institutions and national systems to situate themselves in international and global contexts are just a few of the most important trends of the last decade. Individually and collectively, these developments have exerted important pressures on the core functions of higher education, including teaching and learning. These changes have had significant impact on how and what students learn and the way that knowledge, skills, learning, and teaching are assessed. (Altbach et al. 2009: 111).

As a teacher at a higher learning institution, I subscribe to the paradigm that teaching and learning should, in the main, serve the purpose of solving the many problems of our communities, our country and the world. Students must learn the required skills and analytical tools for contributing towards finding solutions to the many challenges confronting 21st century society. Examples of problems of scale are the burgeoning population growth, climate change, terrorism, economic crisis, environmental degradation, human trafficking, poverty, inequality, crime, abuse against women and children, corruption in both the public and private sectors and, now, the alarming presence of a new virus in society. The key aim, in the case of my module, is for students to be sufficiently informed about the natural environment and South African society. Covid-19 provides a new context for understanding the relationship between human beings and the natural environment. Transitioning to remote teaching also provides the opportunity to attempt to balance teaching with independent learning, such that 'learning for life' becomes a possibility. I will experiment with using more readings than notes as readings may 'fill in the blanks' for the teacher's 'absence'. I intend collecting information on Covid-19 and the natural environment, in order to make teaching and learning more relevant to the present times. In general, much of conventional teaching and learning tends to revolve around the content to be delivered and the teacher. The students are mostly passive listeners, especially in big classes of 350 students and more at any time. Aside from the practical challenges of remote learning, students now have the opportunity to become active learners and learners for life. The opportunity also presents itself for the teacher to tap into the prior knowledge of students. Remote teaching and learning therefore provide an opening to transition from a teacher-centric to a student-centric pedagogy of teaching and learning. In other words, Covid-19 opens up the prospect for teaching and learning to not be focused on the place and the teacher, but on the learning process itself. My experience is that some students do not feel the need to attend lectures unless a register of attendance is taken, and this is not practical in a class of 350 students. Uploading lecture notes before the actual lecture can be described as 'flipping the classroom' approach to teaching and learning. Covering content is an important aspect of the teaching curriculum and one has to find ways to 'get the students ready' for assessments. So that students are not left behind, as a teacher, one also has to prepare for 'catch up sessions'. Covid-19 is a reminder that teaching and learning is a process that is open to change, and one is continuously learning about new ways of teaching and learning. According to Barr and Tagg:

> In its briefest form, the paradigm that has governed our college is this: A college is an institution that exists to provide instruction. Subtly but profoundly we are shifting to a new paradigm: A college is an institution that exists to produce learning. This shift changes everything. It is both needed and wanted (Barr and Tagg 1995: 1).

At the time of writing, the university has been proactive to ensure that teachers and representatives of students are consulted in terms of preparing for the transition to remote teaching and learning. In this regard anxieties and concerns about transitioning were lessened with different types of material support such as data packages being made available. As to whether the quantity of such data is sufficient, only time will tell. In an age where information is unlimited, one can guess that data accessibility is not sufficient, unless it itself is unlimited. Already there are concerns that students' data are not refilled on time. In terms of teaching infrastructure for remote teaching and learning, an online teaching portal has been quickly improved upon and upgraded continuously:

> The Teach Online Portal is intended to be an evolving 'agnostic communal facility' where colleagues share their online resources with the University community. The content is curated by the University Teaching and Learning Office (UTLO) and the Teaching and Learning leadership (UKZN Teaching and Learning Framework – Recovery of the Academic Programme 2020).

A dry-run to test the reliability of remote teaching and learning has been under way. The goals are to test issues of technological, teaching and assessment functionality. More importantly, the dry run was expected to provide some kind of measurement index as to the actual preparedness of the university community to transition to remote teaching and learning. The university has also rolled out various forms of training for teachers, which are certainly a welcome support to move the process forward. With online workshops on teaching, one is being reminded to reimagine teaching and to rethink teaching and learning. One is motivated to rethink the quality of lectures and whether the same standard of teaching conducted in the classroom is applicable to that of remote teaching and learning. In any event, according to Morton (2009: 58), the elements of a good lecture within a classroom setting are:

1. It is delivered in a way that is informative, interesting and engaging.

2. The content is well organised and easy to follow. Students can understand the development of the argument, or the logic in the ordering of the information or ideas.

3. Students feel involved. This may be through some type of active participation, use of relevant examples to which they can relate and by being made to think about what is being said. The ability to

118

engage students through questioning, no matter what the class size, is an important way of getting students involved.

4. Students leave wondering where the time has gone.

5. Students leave knowing that they have learned something(s), and are often inspired to go off and find out more.

If some of the above guidelines can be reproduced with remote teaching and learning then it will be a step in the right direction. Covid-19 and the transition to remote teaching and learning is also allowing one to reflect on one's teaching philosophies. Such reflections are enabled by the workshops on teaching and learning, and communications inviting teachers to contribute to scholarship on the subject, for example, the call for book chapters such as this one and others wishing to: 'explore the teaching of philosophy of education in teacher education programmes at education faculties in South Africa' (Maharajh and Hlatshwayo 2020). The following are some of the principles drawn up by the university with regard to teaching and learning, which seek to guide teachers along the path of remote teaching and learning (UKZN Teaching and Learning Framework 2020: 1):

1. Students should be placed at the centre of all decisions taken and should be consulted in whatever solution is proposed.

2. Equitable and quality access for all students should be foregrounded in our approach.

3. Lectures should as far as possible be broken down into smaller more manageable chunks to limit data usage.

4. Moodle is the official Learning Management Solution of UKZN and all content should be uploaded onto the platform.

5. The intention should be to bring everyone along with us on this journey. Staff and students should be encouraged to contribute and bring forward any ideas to enhance the solution.

Navigating the Transition to Remote Assessment and Grading

History will readily dub the 1990s – as well as the early years of the new millennium – 'the assessment era', when belief in the power of assessment to provide a rational, efficient and publicly acceptable mechanism of judgement and control reached its high point. It is probably no accident that this development came at a time when capitalism itself became transformed into a global system and the other trappings of globalisation – instant international communication and the knowledge economy – also developed in previously almost unimaginable ways, a decade during which email and the World Wide Web for example, have transformed all our lives (Broadfoot and Black 2004: 13).

In the type of society that we live in, what seems to be uppermost in students' minds is whether they will pass at the end of the year. It is an understandable motivation and goal, but need not be the sole purpose of teaching and learning. Thus, we observe that student attendance is at its highest at the start of the semester, when the requirements for the module are communicated and towards the end of the semester when information about assessments, exam logistics and other notices is communicated. Students are aware that lecture material will be posted onto Moodle. Where big classes of students are involved, the taking of a register is both inconvenient and time-consuming and usurps both teaching and learning time. With Covid-19 the issue of 'attending class' becomes that much more fluid and the range of assessments has to be carefully thought through, planned and executed. Universities strive for significant pass rates at the end of the year, especially given the history of education in entrenching apartheid. There are many and varied views and expectations when it comes to assessing students, either for their learning or for their grading. Assessment falls into two main categories, summative and formative. The former is primarily for the purposes of feedback on learning and the latter for the purposes of grading students.

The world is in a social, economic and environmental crisis. My view is that assessing learning should, in the final analysis, contribute towards serving the purpose of solving the many problems of the world. Students must be taught in such ways that they learn and develop the required skills and analytical tools to contribute toward finding solutions to the many challenges confronting 21st century society. The way we assess student learning can help contribute, even in a small way, towards resolving the many problems confronting us. Hence, if in the 21st century, the student is to be at the centre of teaching and learning, then it is educationally sound to ensure that the student is at the centre of the assessment process as well. This should be the fundamental principle underpinning teaching, learning and assessment, because assessment should have as its final goal that of life-long learning and not merely to ascertain whether the student passes or fails. As a species we learn to survive. It is the law of both the animal and the plant kingdom. The highly complex society we live in means that students require assessments in order to reflect on teaching and learning, even if such assessments are usually highly organised, regulated and controlled. Sometimes students become very anxious about assessments in their present form. Learning a new skill, a new task or a new bit of information about something is fundamentally enabling, empowering and is also a confidence builder. Human beings are by nature good learners and in their quest to survive in a highly competitive world, they learn many and varied ways of getting by. But how do we know whether what and how we are learning will have positive or negative impacts for the person, his or her family, his or her community and the world? According to Reeves (2006) no matter the field or discipline, there are a set of meta-outcomes that transcend the domains of cognitive, conative, affective and psychomotor learning. These kinds of meta-outcomes will not be achieved in higher education unless they are meaningfully assessed. The following are some of these outcomes: using information intelligently; communicating skills through various media; demonstrating understanding; being creative; thinking critically; making sound judgements; problem solving; being committed to life-long learning; exhibiting intellectual curiosity; etc. With the massification and bureaucratisation of universities, though, teaching, learning and assessments are also under scrutiny in society's quest for efficiency, speed, standardisation and throughput:

> Regrettably, even within the cognitive domain much more attention is paid to the lower half of the domain (remembering, understating, and applying) than it is to the arguably more important upper half (analysing, evaluating, and creating). This problem stems largely from the relative ease with which the skills encompassed in the lower half can be taught and tested within most fields or disciplines. Teaching and assessing the cognitive skills required for analysis, evaluation, and creation takes more time and effort than many, if not most, university instructors feel they have (Reeves, 2006: 4–6).

With the entry of Covid-19 and a major disruption to the academic calendar and programme, the issue of assessing students for the purposes of grading is fraught with unknown challenges. However, with the university providing some sort of a framework to assess student learning, the field of assessment does not seem too daunting as it was at the beginning of the lockdown. The UKZN College of Humanities Online Continuous Assessment Framework (2020) comprises two main sets of principles seeking to inform assessment going forward:

1. Principles of assessment e.g. reliability, validity, inclusive, equitable, manageable, and others.

2. Principles underpinning continuous online assessment e.g. formative and summative, encourage active learning, and others.

The question of Duly Performed or DP certificates has always been an issue in the College of Humanities, in general, and sociology, in particular. Every year there is pressure on the discipline by the Student representative Council or SRC to waive the DP for the year. With Covid-19 the university understood the challenges of sticking to the DP system in a context of unforeseen circumstances. Based on experience, the university may have also predicted the uproar that could be caused by the students if the DP was to be kept intact. The university has therefore correctly decided to waive the DP for 2020. With the principles and guidelines set out in the College of Humanities Online Continuous Assessment Framework (2020), the university's standards of learning and assessing learning are still intact. Assessments, where applicable, are being moderated by both internal and external moderators. With regard to the principle of quality assurance: 'in keeping with the UKZN assessment policy, lecturers/tutors/markers are to uphold quality assurance principles in terms of the quality of assessments (must test the module outcomes), quality of marking, and plagiarism rules' (UKZN College of Humanities Online Continuous Assessment Framework 2020: 4). However, even with the best of guidelines and planning, our experience in sociology over the years is that some students are not responsive, for one reason or the other, when it comes to assessments. This frustrates teachers and tutors who put in a great deal of work and time to ensure the smooth running of assessments, especially with student numbers as high as 1,600. This is definitely an area of concern, more so within the context of Covid-19 and the transition to remote assessments.

The Human Factor in the Time of Covid-19

Universities are high-pressure environments at the best of times. Under lockdown and the other measures to reduce the spread of Covid-19 – such as physical distancing and reduced social interactions – these pressures are exacerbated ... higher education institutions have become 'increasingly gamified with points and rankings, and winners and losers' and this is a contributing factor to the pressure that academics and professional staff feel in the workplace (Mangolothi and Rippenaar-Moses 2020).

Besides the socio-economic challenges faced by the majority of South Africans, Covid-19 seems to have added another layer to mental health challenges facing many people. The fear and anxiety of contracting Covid-19 and becoming ill and dying is real. The fear and anxiety of someone close to you contracting Covid-19 and becoming ill and dying is real. In fact, at the time of writing colleagues and friends are tragically losing loved ones to Covid-19. Other colleagues are afraid for their children and family members contracting Covid-19 due to schools in the country not being in full readiness to open but have opened nevertheless. We are afraid for ourselves, especially for those of us with underlying health issues. We are afraid for our elder parents and family members with comorbidities and for family members who are on the frontline of Covid-19. The majority, if not all people in South Africa, must be going through similar emotions. Teaching and learning usually take place within a physical space, a space that has become overly risky due to Covid-19. However, whilst the plan is to engage through a virtual medium, under work-pressurised situations, the reality may require persons to be present in the workplace for varied reasons such as the failure of technology in facilitating administrative issues amongst others. This happens within the context of a phased opening of society and as South African society takes risky steps towards moving back into spaces where Covid-19 may be present. The unlocking of movement is also taking place within the very precarious seasons of autumn and winter when different types of colds and flu tend to spike. We seem to be working longer hours and more intensely through remote learning. There do not seem to be sufficient hours in a day. The line between work, me-time and family-time has been all but eliminated. In a staff meeting with the Vice Chancellor, a gloomy outlook of the country's financial situation, in general, and the university's, in particular, was given. It seems with Covid-19 and impending economic recession and even depression, it will be a long process of recovery. As it stands the academic calendar may go into February of 2021 and there's no telling what may happen if the Covid-19 situation worsens: 'we don't know yet whether this wave of infections will be the first and last, or merely the beginning of a rolling crisis for years to come' (Van Onselen 2020: 22). As a teacher, I have to take into consideration that students may find themselves in worse off situations in terms of socio-economic challenges, as well as experiencing anxieties about remote teaching and learning. Some may contract Covid-19 themselves. Some may have family members who will contract Covid-19. Some may lose family members to Covid-19. These are indeed very difficult and scary times as the numbers tend to be going up with time in South Africa. One therefore has to take into consideration the 'human factor' when it comes to teaching and learning, in general, and of assessments, in particular. One has to therefore think through contingency plans for those students that may fall behind for one reason or another. Covid-19 is challenging all that we knew was normal. People in all parts of the world are now talking about the 'new normal'. We in South Africa are continuously engaging with change, mostly emanating from our very difficult history. But Covid-19 has triggered societal change on an unimaginable and somewhat terrifying scale. We are still very much in uncertain times as we do not really know how long Covid-19 will be around. The World Health Organization thinks it may be here to stay. If that is the case, then humanity's only hope is for there to be a vaccine that will immunise humankind against Covid-19. What I have come to realise is that things do not come to a standstill – society's operations must continue. Widespread technology use has also raised concerns about security and privacy issues – as we have learnt when a parliamentary sitting was hacked into (Dipokho 2020). As to whether higher institutions will go back to the 'old normal', only time will tell.

References

Altbach, P., Reisberg, L. and Rumbley, L. (2009) *Trends in Global Higher Education: Tracking an Academic Revolution*, A Report Prepared for the UNESCO, World Conference on Higher Education.

Barr, R. and Tagg, J. (1995) 'From teaching to learning: a new paradigm for undergraduate education', *Change*, Vol. 27, No. 6, pp. 12–26.

Broadfoot, P. and Black, P. (2004) 'Redefining assessment? The first ten years of assessment in education', *Assessment in Education, Principles Policy and Practice*, Vol. 11, No. 1, pp. 7–26.

Communiqué from the office of the Deputy Vice-Chancellor (2020) Teaching and Learning. Online learning resources – UKZN Teach Online Portal, UKZN.

Dipokho, W. (2020) *Parliament's Zoom hack should be a wake-up call*, https://www.iol.co.za/technology/techsperts/parliaments-zoom-hack-should-be-a-wake-up-call-47715979 (accessed 22 October 2020).

Gool, J. (1966) *The Crimes of Bantu Education in South Africa*, Zambia: All African Convention and Unity Movement.

Kayoka, P. (2020) COVID-19: Brace yourself for impact, Department of Agriculture and Animal Health, Unisa.

Maharajh, L. and Hlatshwayo, M. (2020). Book Chapters: Teaching of Philosophy of Education at Universities, UKZN.

Mangolothi, B. and Rippenaar-Moses, L. (2020) 'Academics' health suffers under COVID-19. More than ever, higher education institutions need to look after employees' mental wellbeing', *Mail and Guardian*, 5 June.

Ministry of Health (MOH), South Africa (2020) Daily Covid-19 report.

Morton, Ann (2009) 'Lecturing to large groups', in H. Fry, S. Ketteridge and S. Marshall (eds) *A Handbook for Teaching and Learning in Higher Education: Enhancing Academic Practice*, 3rd edition, New York: Routledge.

Reeves, T. (2006) 'How do you know they are learning? The importance of alignment in higher education', *International Journal of Learning Technology*, Vol. 2, No. 4, pp. 294–309.

UKZN (2020) Teaching and Learning Framework – Recovery of the Academic Programme.

UKZN (2020) College of Humanities Online Continuous Assessment Framework.

UKZN (2020) Student online survey.

Van Onselen, P. (2020) 'Denying unis a lifeline is ideological wilful ignorance – higher education is vital to our future, and not just economically, *The Weekend Australian*, 25 April.

Chapter 7

Complexities of Employing Transformative Pedagogy in Online Teaching in the Covid-19 Era

Evans Shoko
University of KwaZulu-Natal

Introduction

Lockdowns induced by Covid-19 led to serious challenges for both academics and students who had prepared for contact lectures at tertiary institutions worldwide (Adedoyin and Soykan 2020; Ali 2020; Almaiah, Al-Khasawneh and Althunibat 2020; Pokhrel and Chhetri 2021). This disruption led to the adoption of remote-learning strategies at tertiary institutions largely used to contact lectures. Richer countries had the resources to quickly transition to online teaching, although this still required considerable effort (Jiang, Islam, Gu and Spector 2021). However, the situation in middle- to lower-income countries was dire, due to inequalities amplified by Covid-19 and linked to, for example, access to the internet, computers and connectivity issues (Dube 2020). However, many African countries and South Africa, in particular, have managed to solve some of these challenges creatively. For example, according to the Council of Higher Education (CHE 2020) in South Africa, tertiary students were provided with monthly allocations of data (including academics) and laptops (given to first-year National Student Financial Aid Scheme (NSFAS) funded students). Students from the second year upwards had already been allocated laptops in their first years. With the issue of access largely solved, a lingering issue is how academics and students used to physical lectures and congregate settings cope and adapt to online teaching and learning. The current challenge also relates to how academics can best teach subject concepts within an online working environment and the effect on student perspective formation.

The transformative learning approach is conceptualised in this chapter as eminently suitable for online teaching and learning because of its focus on the process of learning as opposed to the memorising of concepts. This approach asserts that students grow cognitively when they contend with 'disorienting dilemmas' – life crises that force them to question their long-held assumptions leading to a transformation of their attitudes and skills considering these reflections (Mezirow 1978). When students scrutinise their experiences vis-à-vis prevailing issues and circumstances, they can act, change and develop a new set of skills. Incorporating transformative education into online teaching and learning is currently critical, where Covid-19 as a 'disorienting dilemma' has forced academics to teach online.

Online learning has exposed challenges relating to access for students. For example, a study by Dube (2020) in South Africa revealed that this mode of learning excludes rural-based students because of a lack of resources for internet connection and low-technology software. Pather et al. (2020) found that although 84,6% of students in their study owned a computer or tablet, 43.9% lacked access to online learning materials and platforms and had to travel to public places to access these. This has necessitated a greater understanding of how to make teaching and learning more inclusive. It is argued in this chapter that comprehending the problems that sustain social inequality as well as different access, becomes important for determining activities to be incorporated into learning strategy for social justice within students' online learning settings.

Considering the Covid-19 challenges to access and connectivity for students, it can seem paradoxical that online teaching may be suitable for transformative education. However, previous research indicates that online class conversations often appear more mutually respectful and informal compared to in-person discussions and, in this way, they challenge conventional conceptions of power that exist within the university classroom (Cuschieri and Colleja Agius 2020; George 2020; Mishra, Gupta and Shree 2020). Donnelly (2017) argued that this somewhat open atmosphere is suitable for teaching methods that critically scrutinise societal designs of power versus dominance. Likewise, Daumiller et al. (2021) have argued that students are frequently more willing to share information such as personal experiences and opinions online, possibly due to the sense of anonymity provided by the online learning environment. This kind of sharing, as well as a sense of cooperative spirit, is also vital for transformative education.

Transformational Learning Theory

Developed by Mezirow (1978: 100), transformative learning theory holds that 'the way learners interpret and reinterpret their sense experience is central to making meaning and hence learning'. The theory begins with a basic proposition that students adjust to new levels of thinking based on new information and thus both academics and students benefit from understanding the effect of different learning modes for the student. Students tend to compare new-found information with their experiences, through critical reflection. Learning thus goes beyond merely getting the knowledge, but goes into how 'learners find meaning in their lives and understanding' (Raikou 2019: 89). This will result in great changes in perceptions as students begin to examine phenomena from new perspectives, providing room for fresh insights and information. However, Mezirow (2018: 115) argued that this requires 'true freedom of thought and understanding'.

Mezirow (1978) divided learning into two categories, i.e., instrumental and communicative learning. In instrumental learning, the stress is on task-focused problem-solving, whereas, in communicative learning, there is a focus on 'how people communicate their feelings, needs, and desires' (Mezirow 2018: 115). These elements are equally important if students are to grasp diverse types of understanding and new perspectives (both emotional and logical) to challenge their prior knowledge. This is supported by Bickmore's (2017) contention that transformative learning occurs when learning moves beyond the mind to connect with the heart and actions and, thus, should be integrated into every subject. In addition, meaning structures (predispositions and assumptions shaping interpretation of information) are also important in transformative learning as they inspire students to scrutinise their beliefs analytically, be immersed in social matters and participate in social activities (Fujino et al. 2018). In this way, students can challenge their own beliefs and perspectives and analyse if they are still true in the current environment.

Key tenets of transformative learning theory were used in this study for an investigation into emerging teaching and learning challenges linked to Covid-19 and the extent to which academics and students cope and find opportunities to advance new modes of learning which are not only content-focused, but also involves the use of novel digital tools. For example, the concept of 'disorienting dilemmas' implies that students discover that what they have learnt in their early life may not be accurate, and this challenges them (Fujino et al. 2018). Prior to 2019 most universities and colleges emphasised physical lectures, rarely considering online classes applicable especially in an African setting, and so the commencement of online learning may have induced a 'disorienting dilemma' to many students. The initial shock may have led to 'self-examination', where students began to reflect on their long-held beliefs and connect them to the 'disorienting dilemma', which can induce changes of perspective (Rapanta et al. 2020). Covid-19 did not only challenge access to educational facilities but beliefs regarding the ability of students to use digital learning tools successfully. This change of perspective is enabled through critical assessment of assumptions, which would enable the academics and their students to 'plan a course of action' which necessitates the learning of new things for this 'plan' to work. New things in the Covid-19 era can include the use of Zoom, Microsoft teams and group online discussions, submission of assignments online and learning while residing in their communities. Students may also start to explore and try new roles, that may bring self-efficacy, through independent working and decision making (Beka 2021).

This study used the transformative learning theory blueprint to construct open-ended questions within a semi-structured interview (Collins and Stockton 2018). The study asked questions relating to how the use of transformative learning in a Covid-19 environment could assist in online teaching and learning and elaborated on specific methods for this. Participants were also asked to provide instances where they would employ these methods, in an online class, and to describe the results. Participants further responded to questions on the types and extent of the use of digital tools in teaching and learning. In addition, they were requested to describe the role of the academic and the students in an online class.

Methodology

The study was carried out at the University of KwaZulu-Natal (UKZN), within the College of Humanities. The college consists of six schools, namely, applied human sciences, arts, built environment and development studies, education and religious, philosophy, classics as well as social sciences. It has 27 research, teaching and learning units. The study's target population were academics working within the college who were teaching online during the data collection phase.

The study used a phenomenological research design which focused on the 'lived experiences' of academics in relation to their use of a transformative approach in online teaching, due to Covid-19 induced lockdowns and social distancing guidelines. A research design using phenomenology explores people's experiences of a phenomenon (Qutoshi 2018). In line with this, the study obtained qualitative narratives on the use of the transformative pedagogy from academics teaching within the College of Humanities at the University of KwaZulu-Natal (UKZN).

Purposive sampling was used to choose potential participants, through posting interview questions on the College of Humanities staff mailing list. The researcher aimed for a sample size of 15, but was guided by the principle of data saturation, which means data was collected to a point where the quantity and quality of information collected were deemed satisfactory. Little new information was collected after 10 participants as they belonged largely to the same analytic 'category'. Open-ended in-depth questions produced rich data and thus, ultimately a smaller sample of 10 participants was deemed sufficient and was suitable for the complex analysis required.

A set of questions was sent to participants by email, with a link to Google Forms and they were given two months to respond. Interviews were conducted during the hard lockdown in South Africa, and to follow Covid-19 regulations regarding social and physical distancing, email interviews were chosen rather than face-to-face meetings. All participants responded with typed responses on Google Forms. Responses were then presented using phenomenological analysis in order to explore the lived experiences of the academics. Their accounts of their teaching experience were analysed to 'explicate an underlying structure in these accounts' (Creswell and Creswell 2017: 29). The intention was to consider how they facilitated transformative learning in a Covid-19 induced and socially distanced online course for students from diverse backgrounds. It was important to hear accounts from academics and then compare these accounts with already published literature to infer conclusions. The study followed ethical guidelines which included obtaining permission from the College of Humanities, ethical clearance from the University of KwaZulu-Natal Humanities Research Ethics Committee, informing the participants about the study, obtaining informed consent and maintaining participant anonymity by using pseudocodes (L1–L10).

Findings and Discussion

The majority of the participants were female (6) and the same number also had masters' degrees (see Table 1).

PARTICIPANT CODE	GENDER	HIGHEST QUALIFICATION	WORK EXPERIENCE
L1	Male	PhD	15
L2	Male	Masters	6
L3	Female	PhD	10
L4	Female	Masters	9
L5	Male	PhD	21
L6	Male	Masters	7
L7	Female	PhD	14
L8	Female	Masters	11
L9	Female	Masters	8
L10	Female	Masters	5

Table 1: Participant characteristics

Narratives from the participants illustrated the great potential of transformative pedagogy in a 'successful' online class and in offsetting the challenges of Covid-19 socially distanced learning. The following suggestions were made and became key sub-topics: generate an enabling environment;

urge the students to reflect on their experiences and biases; use participatory teaching strategies; use practical situations that speak to social inequalities; and assist students to apply an action-oriented problem-solving approach.

Generating an Enabling Environment

Within the context of the Covid-19 disorienting dilemma, which changed traditional face-face into online classes, it was always important for the academic to create an enabling environment for students to challenge their perspectives to learning. One of the key findings from participant narratives was that the foundation of transformative education is the establishment of an enabling online learning environment. This was echoed in propositions by Qutoshi (2018) that an enabling climate with tolerance is essential due to the implied challenges to learners' beliefs that are fundamental to transformative learning. Most participants agreed that academics can generate an enabling and friendly atmosphere by remaining observant to students' feedback on their challenges in using digital learning tools, aiding collaboration and constructive group dialogue over platforms such as WhatsApp groups and Moodle, as well as by being accessible through replying to emails and WhatsApp messages. Thus academics 'feel' as available as if in face-to-face interactions. All participants stressed that academics should offer their curricula as well as positive support during online classes recognising the need for learners' contributions, and respect, including tolerance for different opinions. According to one participant:

> To promote cohesion in an online class, I ask my students to introduce themselves to their classmates in an initial discussion and/or post pictures of themselves. If the online class involves threaded discussions, I develop mutual trust among my students by arranging small groups and appointing facilitators to enhance peer interaction. Frequent online communication among students serves as the foundation of a supportive class community. (L1)

Dialogue is vital in a socially distanced environment because it enables students to cooperate in learning despite being based in different geographical locations. An online setting can be a panacea to collaboration because online lessons do not have constraints of time as well as place. Students can be involved in recurrent lesson debates that take place within the lesson or over several days. Additionally, many students feel more relaxed openly contributing to computer-facilitated interaction than in contact lessons (Christopher, De Tantillo and Watson 2020). Online classes allow learners to participate attentively without disturbance, which is significant for the students at risk of being side-lined in a class owing to their 'gender, race, social class, or even personality style' (Wang, Zhang and Ye 2021: 34).

Enabling peer dialogue can create a basis of trust within online learning leading to students becoming more involved and feeling more connected, as suggested by narratives from academics. Giving the students the chance to network with their peers is potentially beneficial as they share ideas with each other and can respond to peers on a given scenario. Having different backgrounds and experiencing different challenges in the current Covid-19 climate offers an opportunity for hearing diverse voices and experiences. Advocates of transformative education avoid teaching designs that escalate inequalities between academics and their students by remaining conscious of the academics' task in online classes. This was demonstrated by one participant's narrative:

> The way I post my work on Moodle reflects a consistently supportive tone, and I always praise students for their cooperation and support of each other in the WhatsApp group. Furthermore, I engage in a greater amount of personal disclosure than I traditionally used to do in my physical classes. (L2)

This personalisation, notwithstanding physical distance, generates trust and frankness in the occasionally impersonal sphere of online teaching. Generally, the academic's role remains primarily that of an organiser who encourages learners' inquiries and innovations as opposed to the person who offers convincing answers (Ali 2020; Beka 2021). According to one participant, students are cognisant of this too:

> I discovered that students enjoy online more than physical group discussions. They like the openness of the discussions. I put out a topic on Moodle and then let the students talk about it exhaustively and then add my comments at the end. I like that approach because it makes the students think harder about the topic at hand and gets them to understand how they feel about it. Sometimes when an academic intervenes in the process a student may just agree with what the same says because they are the expert. (L3)

Urging the Students to Reflect on Their Experiences and Biases

The Covid-19 situation led to increasing self-examination from the students as they questioned their beliefs in the traditional mode of physical lesson delivery. Written tasks, for example, posted on Moodle, aid students to self-examine, connect with social matters and understand the subject material clearly. To support self-examination academics said they often choose themes that encourage the critical review of students' long-held principles and beliefs as well as permit them to express their views. For example, one academic illustrated how he motivated students through posing a scenario for a group debate on a course in human rights and civic engagement (note how the example is oriented towards the use of online platforms as the 'new normal'):

> Many people have personal beliefs about what human rights, especially regarding privacy and protection against cyber-bullying, how to best apply them, and how and when to provide recourse in the case on faceless social media characters. These beliefs stem from many different sources and are often strongly influenced by cultural experiences. The discussion for this week centres on a series of related questions: What are the main elements of your theory about human rights? What do you believe that governments must do to protect people from cyberbullying? What is the best way to use online platforms to challenge human rights abuses, in your experience? Where do your ideas come from? How do your ideas and experiences connect with or differ from the research and views that the readings present? (L2)

Generally, academics who appreciate transformational learning urge students to contend with their opinions on core problems and assist them to be aware of the cause of their assumptions (Kgari-Masondo and Chimbunde 2021). This 'critical assessment of assumptions' process is flexible and may be utilised to conduct online dialogue in many subjects. An art lecturer provided an example in this regard of a group discussion given to the class:

> What are the guidelines that you use to determine whether an object is an art? Do you believe that certain universal traits of beauty or art transcend opinion, time, and place? Has your definition of art changed during your lifetime? Where do your ideas and views come from? (L4)

Another example was provided by a development studies lecturer:

> Do you believe the use of social media can work for democracy in all societies? Please share your opinion as well as its basis. For example, many students may write about how many democratic revolutions were largely driven on social media, but it is important to also describe why you believe that an engaged citizenry is important or beneficial. Can

social media democracy be exported to countries that lack a history or precedent for this style of civic engagement? (L5)

Another significant component of transformative education is the stimulation of students' understanding of other viewpoints (Coutts 2018). Debates may openly encourage students to consider diverse characteristics of an issue and evaluate the advantages and disadvantages of both sides before asserting their view. These ideas are demonstrated in an example of a dialogue prompt posted on Moodle by a sociology lecturer:

> Whose duty is it to develop the well-being of people residing in poor neighbourhoods? Some emphasise the role of personal responsibility (for example, residents must earn enough money to move to a community that can supply greater resources for themselves and their families); others advocate for greater collective responsibility (that is, the government must redistribute wealth and funding toward poor neighbourhoods to provide greater resources). Explain your thoughts on this issue and consider the advantages and disadvantages of both arguments. (L2)

Like the findings above, arguments by Mascolo (2020) reveal that online teaching allows introspective dialogue to progress slowly for the duration of some days, which may clarify variances in perceptions. In tailored online debates, students equate their beliefs, scrutinise them for uniformities and discrepancies, and cultivate integrative deductions (Corrie, Cunliffe and Hayes 2021). These interchanges can be assisted by online interactions with specialists or discussions with students from other courses or universities. Thus, the central argument in this chapter is that in an online class, it is important to let students regularly engage in constant dialogues about contentious topics and explore different views as articulated by their colleagues.

Participatory Online Teaching Strategies

Transformative pedagogy supposes that students are dynamically engaged in the class and academics frequently employ strategies that include collaborative scholarship. This contrasts with the so-called banking standard of instruction, whereby academics mostly trust lecturers and believe that students are passive recipients of evidence in the learning process (Raikou 2019). Transformative education, conversely, ensues when students feel a duty to add to the lesson, feel enabled and trust that their opinions matter (Herbert, Baize-Ward and Latz 2018).

135

Participant narratives point towards the fact that online teaching often inspires students to become self-reliant and have self-efficacy. For instance, one participant stressed the effectiveness and importance of analysis of case reports and other storylines, which expands students' engagement and improves their relational empathy (L3). This method may include reading memoirs, text or related newspaper coverage. Similarly, another participant insinuated that students in online-based courses examine cases in a cooperative way by using apparatuses such as university-based emails, WhatsApp groups, Moodle debates and Zoom discussions (L1). Within online classes, students can also listen to video or audio-recorded streams that describe actual experiences of different people, for example, a migrant's experiences during Covid-19 lockdowns, living conditions and drug-related problems of the homeless (L2). Other contact lesson approaches that challenge students' assumptions and encourage the implementation of other viewpoints can be adjusted for online usage. Corresponding with the above findings, Mittal, Mantri, Tandon and Dwivedi (2021) explained how to employ unsynchronised Moodle discussion to enable students' discussions. Within this adjustment, one learner defends a viewpoint, while a second learner becomes a critic. Placements on Moodle allow sequential articulation and contradiction which then offer written evidence of the conversation. These results are wholly in harmony with the stress on student decision making encouraged by advocates of transformative education (Coutts 2018; Manan 2020; Ovens 2017; Pavlou 2020). Countless teaching approaches that aspire to increase student participation within online settings are adjustments of contact lecture techniques.

Online teaching provides the chance to employ internet kits that may not be readily accessible for face-to-face teaching. All participants agreed that academics can have students not merely read material on the internet but post some evidence online to encourage learner cooperation and participation (L4). For example, Moodle discussions allow students to post their responses promptly online and afford the chance for peers to counter. This acts somewhat like weblogs (although not popular in African universities) which can receive programmed information pods from news sites and additional websites that convey class topics to inform dialogue (Arani 2020; Poudel and Singh 2020). Likewise, academics teaching online classes can utilise wikis permitting students to cooperate in the construction and proofreading of documents as well as online web pages (Hudson 2018; Steen and Wache 2017). These kits and related online products can produce significant levels of learner collaboration, participation and collaborative production of know-how.

Using Practical Situations that Speak to Social Inequalities

Covid-19 has led to the magnification of inequalities, some of which were latent in South Africa. There has been an extensive circulation of videos purportedly showing the police as well as South Africa National Defence Forces members beating black people for contravention of the lockdown regulations, while white people were shown doing fitness runs and braaiing (Newzroom Afrika 15 April 2020). In this case, transformative education can magnify students' consciousness of how social forces impact citizens. This inquiry often includes awareness raising and recognising the reality of oppression. Connecting programme subject matter to social and political questions as exemplified above may be direct in some subjects but equivalents can be less evident in some courses. Generally, academics can address general inequalities by judiciously probing the subject data in their online classes. Academics can also scientifically consider the impact of 'culture, race, social class, gender, sexual orientation, age, or disability on the material in use' (Beech 2021: 74). For example, one participant (L1), a psychology lecturer, said he presented scientific evidence about the genetic basis of the race then detailed the health attention inequalities that happen due to race. The lecturer then prompted students to do a cooperative online tutorial on race created by a particular website. A culture and media studies lecturer (L3) depicted the imaging of gays as well as lesbians in the television and the film industry over the last 50 years to assess terminologies of stigma or wider social tolerance. The students then watched and studied films analytically that are publicly available as well as current telenovelas utilising online videos. A sociology lecturer (L2) analysed how transformations in government laws regarding drug crimes have helped to amplify the imprisonment rate of drug pushers. Students then used prison convict search locators accessible online to study sentencing configurations for crimes on a province-by-province basis.

The above topics all speak to core societal justice topics, that have been amplified by Covid-19: inclusion vs exclusion, equality in resource allocation and prospects, as well as the influence of socially reinforced authority and a chain of command. To encourage transformative education in online classes, academics need to select readings as well as cultivate deliberations that centre on how a country's governance culture influences access. Students can use online materials to examine how political arrangements shape access to employment.

Action-oriented Problem-solving Approach

Transformative education can involve a series of interchanges that depend on lecturers encouraging student reflection and assisting them to act to promote collective good (Collay 2017). Academics can encourage students to advance the skills required to contribute to an equal society and become mediators for social transformation (Vallance and Towndrow 2018). Thus, social action may take various forms for university students. For instance, one participant (L9) explained an assignment in which each learner selected a social question related their interests to a civic cluster, contributed to a local venture, formed a speech conference to enlighten others and then, finally, analysed their venture through a presentation to the online class.

Some participants argued that academics using transformative pedagogy can use their online tasks to engender social transformation that happens outside of traditional class conventional times, for example, penning advocacy commentaries to community or campus newspapers, generating, or partaking in related extra-curricular or community activities, or organising rallies within student communities. Furthermore, online resources can expedite advocacy by assisting students to gain required information, encouraging interaction and facilitating harmonisation with peers who have related interests. To improve the consciousness of social as well as policy matters in an online lesson, students can study online newspaper items that are selected weekly about linked current incidents (L10). Furthermore, they can utilise the internet to research parliamentary debates on human rights. Students can be encouraged to search keywords pertinent to subject content to establish their advocacy schema. Students can also be prompted to correspond through social media, such as Twitter and Facebook, with their lawmakers to advocate for or oppose policies. Social media conversations allow students to assert their opinion on the matter using their understanding from the module and this can work as a stimulus for online lesson discussion. It is argued in this chapter that students can be empowered by this process by evaluating the situation in their community on how policy, as well as socio-economic situations, affect development. This assists them in identifying where and how they may create change (Coutts 2018; Manan 2020; Ovens 2017; Pavlou 2020).

This type of task is highly adaptable for utilisation across subjects. For example, public policy and peace studies students can interact about immigration strategy; economics students can explore laws linked to employment, income or, even, tax plans; psychology scholars can encourage mental health care reorganisation; education students can enunciate their opinions on school subsidy plans or national pass rates; environmental science students can campaign for the safeguarding of the environment or push for renewable energy programmes; and gender studies students can encourage lawmakers to finance women's healthcare plans or foster effective programmes (Hudson 2018).

Conclusion

The Covid-19 pandemic led to the migration of teaching and learning from physical to online classes. Regulations related to Covid-19 lockdowns and the need to ensure safety led to physical distancing in which academics and students were confined to their homes but continued with classes online. There have been challenges to coping and adaptation related to the need to acclimatise to this 'new normal'. Notwithstanding Covid-19, online teaching has demonstrated the potential for enabling students to cooperate or network with classmates and with academics. Using the transformational learning approach can deeply and considerately change students' outlooks and investigative skills to enable their development, both through traditional and/or online design. At the end of the transformational courses, students ideally are more familiar with the content and have an increased worldview, more compassion, enhanced self-awareness, as well as a dedication to being change agents. A transformational learning approach assists students to cooperate, generate an open atmosphere, share opinions, replicate their experiences as well as explore other viewpoints. In the context of Covid-19, it is therefore important to provide every resource (such as data, laptops) and chance to learn (network coverage and student sharing), tasks that challenge social inequalities amplified by Covid-19 to enable the students to form polished opinions, as well as to accept students' convictions and let them communicate through their actions. Every facet of transformative pedagogy commits students to employ critical inquiry together with their individual prior experiences to engage in social concerns that need to be reformed or changed. Conclusively, instead of acting as an obstacle to the use of transformative education, online learning may be an exceedingly effective channel for this approach to teaching as well as student learning. Finally, online teaching offers countless tools to expedite networking, teamwork, information trade-offs and, ultimately, aids students to examine their conjectures analytically, look for additional views, contend with social questions and generate change.

References

Adedoyin, O. B. and Soykan, E. (2020) 'Covid-19 pandemic and online learning: the challenges and opportunities', *Interactive Learning Environments*, pp. 1–13.

Ali, W. (2020) 'Online and remote learning in higher education institutes: A necessity in light of COVID-19 pandemic', *Higher Education Studies*, Vol. 10, No. 3, pp. 16–25.

Almaiah, M. A., Al-Khasawneh, A. and Althunibat, A. (2020) 'Exploring the critical challenges and factors influencing the E-learning system usage during the COVID-19 pandemic', *Education and Information Technologies*, Vol. 25, No. 6, pp. 5261–5280.

Arani, J. A. (2020) 'Teaching reading and writing through a web-based communicative medium: Weblog', *International Journal of Internet Education*, Vol. 19, No. 1, pp. 5–15.

Beech, E. (2021) 'Towards a conceptual model for biblical transformative online learning', *Innovating Christian Education Research*, pp. 73–86.

Beka, A. (2021) 'Transformative school initiative through the use of digital technologies in Kosovo during Covid-19', *Ilkogretim Online–Elementary Education Online*, Vol. 20, No. 1, pp. 851–860.

Bickmore, K. (2017) 'Conflict, peace-building, and education: Rethinking pedagogies in divided societies, Latin America, and around the world', *Comparative and International Education: Issues for Teachers*, Vol. 2, pp. 268–299.

Christopher, R., De Tantillo, L. and Watson, J. (2020) 'Academic caring pedagogy, presence, and communitas in nursing education during the COVID-19 pandemic, *Nursing Outlook*, Vol. 68, No. 6, pp. 822–829.

Collay, M. (2017) 'Transformative learning and teaching: How experienced faculty learned to teach in the on-line environment', *Journal of Transformative Learning*, Vol. 4, No. 2, pp. 21–24.

Collins, C. S. and Stockton, C. M. (2018) 'The central role of theory in qualitative research', *International Journal of Qualitative Methods*, Vol. 17, No. 1, pp. 1–10.

Corrie, I., Cunliffe, E. and Hayes, C. (2021) 'Acknowledging emotive response and epistemic positionality: Disruptive transformative pedagogy amidst a global pandemic', *Journal of Transformative Learning*, pp. 46–51.

Council on Higher Education (CHE) (2020) *Quality Assurance Guidelines for Emergency Remote Teaching and Learning and Assessment During the COVID-19 Pandemic in 2020*, https://www.che.ac.za/#/moreitemdetails (accessed 8 February 2022).

Coutts, L. (2018) 'Selecting motivating repertoire for adult piano students: A transformative pedagogical approach', *British Journal of Music Education*, Vol. 35, No. 3, pp. 285–299.

Creswell, J. W. and Creswell, J. D. (2017) *Research Design: Qualitative, Quantitative, and Mixed Methods Approaches*, Sage: Newbury Park.

Cuschieri, S. and Agius, J. C. (2020) 'Spotlight on the shift to remote anatomical teaching during Covid-19 pandemic: Perspectives and experiences from the University of Malta', *Anatomical Sciences Education*, Vol. 13, No. 6, pp. 671–679.

Daumiller, M., Rinas, R., Hein, J., Janke, S., Dickhäuser, O. and Dresel, M. (2021) 'Shifting from face-to-face to online teaching during COVID-19: The role of university faculty achievement goals for attitudes towards this sudden change, and their relevance for burnout/engagement and student evaluations of teaching quality', *Computers in Human Behavior*, No.118, 106677.

Donnelly, R. (2017) 'Blended problem-based learning in higher education: the intersection of social learning and technology', *Psychosociological Issues in Human Resource Management*, Vol. 5, No. 2, pp. 25–50.

Dube, B. (2020) 'Rural online learning in the context of COVID 19 in South Africa: Evoking an inclusive education approach, *REMIE: Multidisciplinary Journal of Educational Research*, 10, No. 2, pp. 135–157.

Fujino, D. C., Gomez, J. D., Lezra, E., Lipsitz, G., Mitchell, J. and Fonseca, J. (2018) 'A transformative pedagogy for a decolonial world', *Review of Education, Pedagogy, and Cultural Studies*, Vol. 40, No. 2, pp. 69–95.

George, M. L. (2020) 'Effective teaching and examination strategies for undergraduate learning during COVID-19 school restrictions', *Journal of Educational Technology Systems*, Vol. 49, No. 1, pp. 23–48.

Herbert, K. J., Baize-Ward, A. and Latz, A. O. (2018) 'Transformative pedagogy with innovative methodology: using photovoice to understand community college students' needs', *Community College Journal of Research and Practice*, Vol. 42, No. 7-8, pp. 536–549.

Hudson, J. (2018) 'Using Wikis for collaborative writing in the ELT classroom', *International Journal of Pedagogy and Teacher Education*, Vol. 2, No. 2, pp. 413–426.

Jiang, H., Islam, A. Y. M., Gu, X. and Spector, J. M. (2021) 'Online learning satisfaction in higher education during the COVID-19 pandemic: A regional comparison between Eastern and Western Chinese universities', *Education and Information Technologies*, Vol. 26, No. 6, pp. 6747–6769.

Manan, S. A. (2020) 'Teachers as agents of transformative pedagogy: Critical reflexivity, activism and multilingual spaces through a continua of biliteracy lens', *Multilingua*, https://doi.org/10.1515/multi-2019-0096.

Mascolo, M. (2020) 'Transforming higher education: responding to the coronavirus and other looming crises', *Pedagogy and the Human Sciences*, Vol. 7, No. 1, p. 2.

Mezirow, J. (1978) 'Perspective transformation', *Adult Education*, Vol. 28, No. 2, pp. 100–110.

Mezirow, J. (2018) 'Transformative Learning Theory', in K. Illeris (ed.) *Contemporary Theories of Learning*, London: Routledge, pp. 114–128.

Mishra, L., Gupta, T. and Shree, A. (2020) 'Online teaching-learning in higher education during lockdown period of COVID-19 pandemic', *International Journal of Educational Research Open*, No. 1, pp. 1–8.

Mittal, A., Mantri, A., Tandon, U. and Dwivedi, Y. K. (2021) 'A unified perspective on the adoption of online teaching in higher education during the COVID-19 pandemic', *Information Discovery and Delivery*, pp. 117–132.

Newzroom Afrika. (2020) 'SANDF says it will do everything it can to protect South Africans during the coronavirus pandemic', 15 April, https://www.youtube.com/watch?v=hL9BJ6GT2lY (accessed 25 August 2021).

Ovens, A. (2017) 'Putting complexity to work to think differently about transformative pedagogies in teacher education', *Issues in Teacher Education*, Vol. 26, No. 3, pp. 38–51.

Pavlou, V. (2020) 'Art technology integration: Digital storytelling as a transformative pedagogy in primary education', *International Journal of Art & Design Education*, Vol. 39, No. 1, pp. 195–210.

Pokhrel, S. Chhetri, R. (2021) 'A literature review on impact of COVID-19 pandemic on teaching and learning', *Higher Education for the Future*, Vol. 8, No. 1, pp. 133–141.

Poudel, A. P. and Singh, R. K. (2020) 'University Teachers' Use of Blogs for Enhancing the Writing Skills of Students', in E. Carm, M. Johannesen, B. Chandra, L. Øgrim and P. Phyak (eds) *Innovative Technologies and Pedagogical Shifts in Nepalese Higher Education*, USA: Brill, pp. 119–148.

Qutoshi, S. B. (2018) 'Phenomenology: A philosophy and method of inquiry', *Journal of Education and Educational Development*, Vol. 5, No. 1, pp. 215–222.

Raikou, N. (2019) 'Teacher Education at the forefront: Long-term study through the prism of university pedagogy and transformative learning theory', *European Journal of Education Studies*, Vol. 6, No. 3, pp. 88–101.

Rapanta, C., Botturi, L., Goodyear, P., Guàrdia, L. and Koole, M. (2020) 'Online university teaching during and after the Covid-19 crisis: Refocusing teacher presence and learning activity', *Postdigital Science and Education*, Vol. 2, No. 3, pp. 923–945.

Steen, T. and Wache, D. (2017) 'University students' experiences of their use of wikis in collaborative learning', *Open Journal of International Education*, Vol. 2, No. 1, pp. 24–43.

Vallance, M. and Towndrow, P. A. (2018) 'Mapping Computational Thinking for a Transformative Pedagogy', in M. S. Khine (ed.) *Computational Thinking in the STEM Disciplines*, Cham: Springer, pp. 301–325.

Wang, K., Zhang, L. and Ye, L. (2021) 'A nationwide survey of online teaching strategies in dental education in China', *Journal of Dental Education*, Vol. 85, No. 2, pp. 128–134.

Printed in the United States
by Baker & Taylor Publisher Services